Deepening Love, Sex & Intimacy

A True Story

Graham Meltzer

"Fantastic! One of the last largely unexplored frontiers of humanity."   Geoffrey Colwill

"A wonderful read! A book of courage, depth and struggle."   John Croft

"I have…been moved almost to tears by the intensity of the love and truth."   Michael Bailey

"A beautiful and inspiring story. Great reading."
                                    Colin G Smith

"A well-written well-spring of inspiration for those people who seek to heal the world through healing themselves and their ways of relating."
                                    Tom Keily

ISBN-10: 1720539847
ISBN-13: 9781720539841

DEDICATION

To love

CONTENTS

PREFACE

This is a true and very personal story about me, Graham, and Saritha (not her real name)[1] and our love affair that unfolded between April and November, 2014. The setting is the well-known Findhorn spiritual community in North Scotland. We first came together at a party shortly before Saritha planned to leave Findhorn and continue on her journey. We believed we had just over a month to explore being in relationship together. We decided to go for it; to fearlessly dive deep into love, sex and intimacy – to push as far as we could beyond the boundaries of our comfort zones in the limited time available. For we believe that it's 'in that field, out beyond ideas of wrongdoing and rightdoing' (Rumi) that growth and learning occur.

We conceived a project – a project in *conscious* relationship, which we based on a social technology called Dragon Dreaming (DD), described by its creator, John Croft, as 'unconditional love in action.'[2] DD, says Croft, 'offers methods for the realisation of creative, collaborative and sustainable projects.' Our project was certainly to be creative

---

[1] This story is true in every detail but for a few changes of name to protect the privacy of particular individuals.

[2] See http://www.dragondreaming.org/

and collaborative. Sustainable? Perhaps not. Our month-long project ultimately became a seven month long journey, one that was rich, intense, engaging and thought-provoking. In the concluding months the project morphed into an exploration of polyamoury or 'free love.' Or, as Saritha would describe it, 'new ways of being in relationship for the planetary transition based on love, trust and transparency.' This phase was similarly rich, intense, engaging and thought-provoking, but also *very* challenging.

I, Graham, benefited from an enormous amount of personal growth in those seven months, something for which I'll be eternally grateful. The learning has been of my inner life – my emotions and long-standing (sometimes unhealthy) behaviour patterns. I'm a much changed person with a quite different understanding of myself than I had previously. Plus, I've had a ball! The experience has been truly extraordinary. It's rekindled my love of life (which was anyway very strong), fired up my passion and expanded my consciousness. I wish to publicly thank Saritha for taking this journey with me and, indeed, (as you will read) for being my muse, my confidant and my mentor in matters of the heart.

This book was written entirely by me. It takes the form of a diary, *my* diary. Saritha has, of course, read it and has no objection to any of the content. But it's my version of events, not hers; I don't doubt that she would offer a quite different take. The documentation of our relationship began in fact, as a diary, then became a blog and was finally, turned into a book.[1] That I did all of the writing is incidental as far as I'm concerned. I feel that Saritha was equally a collaborator. Her contribution was perhaps of even greater significance, given that she injected most of the ideas, the impetus and the inspiration into our project. Furthermore, I did 90% of the writing 'in the zone;' the words flowed to the keyboard effortlessly and uncensored, without mental exertion, without

---

[1] This explains the occasional changes of tense (from past to present and back again) and the sometimes unconventional verb conjugation.

even much thought. I was a channel for the documenting of our story, simply a channel.

We feel that it's a story worth telling, because we see that most relationships begin without much consciousness and continue to drift rather than be steered. As a result, the potential for depth of experience, learning and growth is self-limiting and never much tapped. Too often, intimate relationships founder or fail for want of any understanding about how to do them better; how to infuse greater consciousness. We hope this book can be a source of ideas and inspiration for others. We thank you for reading and wish you well in your own adventures in loving.

Note: Be warned that some of the content of this book is very sexually explicit. Please do not read on if it is likely to offend.

BEGINNINGS

Diary entry, May 5th, 2014

We met in the hot tub, one dark, momentous night in March – Saritha, me and a friend – a threesome of sorts, with Saritha being the shared object of our keen masculine attention; somewhat competitively, it must be said. She was obscured from my view by darkness. My impressions of her were based on the softness of her languid voice, the feel of her smooth skin and well-toned calf (I gave her an underwater foot massage) and most of all, the stories she told of her life – a life well lived. Intelligent and self-confident, sassy and sensual, she triggered a longing in me that lingered for days.

We next met at a party in the Community Centre (CC).[1] Sitting beside her momentarily, but without recognition (I hadn't really seen her face in the hot tub), I asked her name. "Saritha," she said, which made me laugh and spontaneously prompted that famous chat up line, "Oh hi, I didn't recognise you with your clothes on." She laughed too. It was a sweet moment. We didn't engage much that night. I'm shy with

---

[1] The Community Centre at Findhorn is used mostly for dining. We serve meals there for up to 200 people at a time, but occasionally, it is used for parties, meetings and performances.

women, especially beautiful women, and a lousy flirter. Anyway, she seemed to be in a quiet, private kind of space, dancing and engaging with others, but seemingly reflective and withdrawn.

Our third encounter was at another party in the CC, perhaps a week later. The date was April 19th. We were both dancing. This time her dancing seemed more energetic and she appeared more open. We chatted to the side of the dance floor. Again, I felt shy, and was on the point of leaving the party when she held me back, encouraging me to stay. I suddenly felt more forward, as if she had made the first move. I said I'd stay for a kiss. She said, "Well let's find you one. There are many women here tonight." "But…" I said, "… I only have eyes for you" – another sadly unoriginal and clichéd chat up line. We hugged and cuddled and then moved toward the tea-making area for water. That is where it happened – our first kiss – and what a kiss! Deep, soft, sensual, wet and wonderful; both my brain and my heart exploded in an instant.

We spent what must have been two or three hours snogging passionately, first in the tea area and then on the couch. We didn't hold back; we were very demonstrative. I was completely gone, oblivious to all else. I was lost in a sea of sensuality, sinking and melting into unfathomable softness – entering into the very core of another. In that short time, which seemed like an eternity, I lost my heart to this woman.

FOREPLAY

May 10th, 2014

May 10th, 2014

We spent some days deepening our connection, without being overtly sexual. It seemed right to take it slow and gentle – getting to know each other through talking, sharing, cuddling and caressing. We only had about 10 days before Saritha had to go south for three weeks. So there was hesitancy, mostly on her part, to engage too sexually, too quickly. For me, this was hard, being as sexually driven as I am, as I have been all my life, but I was enjoying the journey, the anticipation and the slow seduction. And also, I was a mess: constantly with butterflies in my gut; distracted at work; unable to think of anything else but her. I'd 'fallen in love;' I *was* 'in love.' But she was not, she made that clear. And she was jokingly disdainful of my being so. That's ok, I thought. I can handle this being one-sided, for the moment anyway. Let's see what develops. Either she'll soften into love or we're on borrowed time.

After some days, we spent a night in bed, then another, then several more. Our love-making was passionate, exploratory and exhilarating, but not penetrative. Saritha was reluctant to go there, to fully surrender before she went away. I was of course frustrated – 'desperate' even, I remember saying – but also very much enjoying the tease, the

6

anticipation, the seeking and the search. And I could imagine how another month of waiting would render the eventual moment of total union that much more profound and meaningful. I was so deeply enjoying being lover, being loved, being 'in love,' that anything seemed possible, everything seemed perfect and right. We made delicious love on an energetic plane. Through touching, caressing, breathing, whispering, imagining and connecting. We'd use our seemingly equally strong sexual energy to build waves of deep orgasmic pleasure – purring, moaning, groaning, yelping in unison to reach a climax that flowed back into moaning purring and stillness. Such energetic lovemaking I've never experienced before. What a revelation. What a trip!

HIATUS

May 23rd, 2014

Saritha's three weeks away really challenged me. The relationship seemed so nascent, so delicate, so unformed. It felt fragile. Communication was sometimes difficult. We mixed modes – texting, calling and Skyping. I found all of them unsatisfactory in that all I really wanted to do was hold her – to gaze into her eyes and feel her skin under my fingertips. My vulnerability was tested even further as it quickly became clear that she was much less of a romantic than me and less inclined to respond to text messages and other means of communication. At times she felt remote. At other times, resistant. She said she was anxious about getting too attached and that, anyway, she was looking for new ways of being in relationship. Now that I know more about her (and about her prior love affair), I understand this better, but at the time, it was hard to hear. I was also very happy for her as she was doing the work about which she's passionate – being an eco-warrior in the world – helping to build community where help is needed. She was enjoying good numbers at presentations and receiving positive feedback and invitations to additional meetings and consultations. This filled my heart with pride and joy. I felt inspired and grateful for the gift of journeying, even if only for a brief moment in time, with a woman of substance – or to quote Hemingway, 'a truly great woman, one that deserves the utmost respect in this world.'

I say, 'if just for a moment,' because I believed our relationship would probably not have a future beyond the end of June when Saritha was intending to travel first to Germany, then Spain, then Portugal, then who knows where. Her residency options in the UK were limited and more importantly, she's a woman on a quest – to fulfil her potential in service to the world. As for me, I'm committed to remaining in my community for the moment, indeed with much the same motivation, i.e. to help build a better world from there. So there was serious doubt about our long-term prospects. Yet, in another way, her plans to leave and travel brought a beautiful added dimension to our relationship – a certain jewel-like preciousness. It felt as if it might be a brief but brilliant shared moment in time – a unique opportunity for a pressure-cooked meeting of hearts, minds and souls.

Saritha's return from Brighton was delayed a few days and then a day more as she, then we, struggled to make travel bookings in a timely fashion. I felt she was on some level, holding back from committing to coming back. She'd not been able to book online, then postponed booking, then been frustrated again. She talked of another festival she'd like to attend on the weekend. Part of me, the anxious and insecure me, was half expecting her to say she was staying on there indefinitely. In the end, I precipitated the booking. I'd have paid any amount to bring her back by any means available and would have unhesitatingly paid £300 for a flight. In the end, she graciously agreed to take a Megabus for £38 – a saving which, in my more sane moments, I really appreciated.

RECONNECTION

May 25th, 2014

I picked her up in Inverness. I was anxious. I remembered how my previous lover would often need time to reconnect when arriving home after a period away. Would it be the same with Saritha? But with the first sight, the first smile and the first kiss, I knew immediately that all would be well; all anxiety melted away. It felt so comfortable driving back home, me with one hand on her thigh, some quiet chat and soft laughter. I was falling in love with this wondrous creature all over again. She moved in with me that night, taking up residence in my wee house in the woods – a house designed for a couple, for lovers, for two souls deepening their relationship – yet it hadn't really been used as such for a few years. What joy I felt at the prospect of living with this woman with whom I was already in love, even though she was still being clear that she was not 'in love' with me. I was ok with the imbalance, and hopeful.

Our lovemaking resumed where it left off: strong, passionate, exploratory, exhilarating and wonderful, but not penetrative – "Not yet," she said. Full and total union would have to wait a little longer, until the time was right, perhaps until I truly won her heart. We talked about creating a ritual to precede our first full fuck and decided, well actually Saritha did, that the coming new moon would be an ideal time. Fortunately, the new moon fell in a day or two. Not long. And, I couldn't wait.

DREAMING

May 28th, 2014

Saritha had several times talked of us making agreements and setting protocols and she'd talked about us 'designing' our month together. At the time I thought, 'Ok, I can go with that.' Having been in open relationships for over 10 years, I was familiar with certain kinds of agreements around transparency and respect, but really had no idea of what she had in mind. I was soon to find out.

Saritha introduced me to Dragon Dreaming at first opportunity. She laid out a mandala on the living room floor using fabric, ribbons, cards and a candle. It was configured in quadrants representing the four phases: Dreaming, Planning, Doing and Celebrating and aligned with the cardinal directions. It had all manner of further dimensions and complexities to it. Then she explained it to me, as she danced around it in a rarefied mode of being that I'd not previously witnessed – part teacher, part mystic, part conjurer – I was entranced, and of course, fell in love with her all over again.

Dragon Dreaming (as I understand it) is a practice, a structure, a methodology and a technology for managing projects, particularly collaborative projects. It's designed for enabling and empowering teams of two or more. Saritha's proposal was that we use it to design a 'container' for our project – the upcoming month of deepening in conscious relationship, deepening in love. I was curious of course; I love a good technology. And I was a little sceptical; I had trouble reconciling the hard science of the technology with the soft socio-spirituality of our project. But I'll try anything once and sought to suspend my disbelief to give this thing a chance. So we started, as one does with DD, by setting an intention for the project. With Saritha's gentle encouragement and prompting, we devised the following:

INTENTION:
We intend to create a one month long safe container for our relationship that serves each of us individually and together as well as our community and the Earth.

We moved quickly into the next phase, Dreaming, whereby we were to dream into our aspirations, our highest ambitions and ideals for the project. We took turns to speak our dreams for the upcoming month together, with Saritha representing herself as well as the Earth and me representing myself and Community. This was the result:

DREAMING
Community: It (the project) seeks in community, the role of supporter and mirror.
Graham: It needs to have peace, joy and rest as significant elements.
Earth: It serves as a conduit for greater connection with nature.
Saritha: It allows me to build trust and to be myself.
Community: It enables each of us, individually and together, to be present in the community.
Graham: It enables and supports deep sharing.
Earth: That this process promotes love... expanding in all directions.
Saritha: It holds a set of principles that are easy to remember and promotes safety, love and trust.
Community: That the love that is created ripples out into the community.
Graham: That what happens inside the bubble enables me to expand into and be more effective in the world.

Earth: That the project serves as an example and inspiration for others to follow.

Saritha: That it includes the support of the community – specifically my women's group.

Community: That the project infuses the community with love and compassion. That the taboo surrounding sex and intimacy is breeched; people will speak more openly about it.

Graham: That the project enables transparency and the permeability of personal boundaries.

Earth: That the project enables us to be an integral part of the Earth; a way for the Earth/Universe to make love with itself – the integration of the sacred feminine/masculine.

Saritha: That it's a channel for inspired action. That we can engage in inspired action together.

Community: That the project brings healing to this community.

Graham: That it enables us to dive deeply into intimacy and union.

Saritha: That we have a safe space to work with our shadows with joy.

Graham: That our lovemaking be safe but also exploratory and through both safety and adventure, we take a journey.

Saritha: That we enjoy each moment of the journey and have a clearer view of next steps.

Graham: That the project become a base for a lifetime friendship.

Saritha: That it creates a new paradigm of how to be in a relationship and that we record and present our findings in a simple and effective manner.

Graham: That we inspire each other moment-to-moment and grow mutual respect.

Saritha: That we find creative ways to work on our project, given the busyness of our schedules

Graham: That we grow kindness.

Saritha: That our learning sheds new light on our awareness of what relationships are.

Graham: That we cultivate fun, laughter and joy.

Saritha: That we spend the month in the flow.

Saritha: That I find a way to dedicate time to Graham and other relationships in a balanced way.

Graham: That in this month, we consciously develop and attain a state of unconditional love for each other and, through that, for all beings.[1]

Wow! I thought, what an amazing, beautiful and ambitious inventory of aspirations. It seemed that in just the hour or two of working on designing our container, we had significantly and profoundly gone where no prior relationship of mine had ever gone before. I was hooked already on the DD concept and the process. And I was beginning to glimpse the rich possibilities of the next month's cohabitation with this wondrous creature.

---

[1] This last one was added retrospectively.

RITUAL

May 30th, 2014

A couple of days passed leading up to our planned ritual on the night of the new moon – beautiful days of deep conversation, cuddling on the couch, cooking and eating simple, nourishing meals, and some of the best sex I have ever enjoyed. The ritual was profound. I had designed the qualities of a sacred space into the bedroom of my house; that it be a temple of sorts. With its cubic volume, minimalist aesthetic, natural light, views and artwork, it's a space conducive to psychological and spiritual nurture – sound sleep, deep meditation and perhaps, tantric sex practices. For the first time really, it was about to be used for the latter purpose. We adorned it with flowers, candles and an altar. Saritha dressed in a beautiful sarong I had just given her; she looked stunning.

We began by making vows, which we wrote individually then read to each other. They went as follows:

VOWS
Graham:
> *I seek in the next month:*
> *– to know and be known*
> *– to see and be seen*

— to hold and be held
— to love and be loved.
I seek deep and mutual understanding.
I seek flow in a river of our own making, one with:
— still ponds of bliss and tranquillity,
— gushing rapids of laughter and joy, and
— swirling eddies of learning and growth.
Ultimately, I seek a state of unconditional love…
— a love that will endure no matter where we are or what we're doing
— a love free from fear
— a love free of expectation
— a love free of judgment, and
— a love infused with understanding, kindness and mutual support.
I seek:
— a love for the ages
— a love that transcends limitations of space and time
— a love that is divine.

Saritha:

*May this month be a journey from who we are now to the
best we can be.*

*May we feel safe and trusting to shed the layers that cover our
true nature.*

*May we live together in mutual respect, empathy and clear
communication, conducive of the expansion of our hearts
and minds.*

*May we spend stimulating and joyful time that feeds
unconditional love.*

*May the passion of our erotic connection be transformed in
the fire of sacred union, beyond our human limitations,
towards our divine essence.*

Having heard each other's vows and feeling confirmed in
their similarity of tone, feeling and intent, we proceeded with
a ritual from a book on Tantra that I'd had on the shelf for
years, but never much referenced. The process was a little
clunky as we were reading and following instructions directly

from the book as we proceeded through the sequence of meditations, blessings and energetic exchanges. And yet, it was beautiful and powerful, as was the quality of the total sexual union that followed – ecstatic, strong and deeply moving, carrying us to new heights of connection and communion.

UNION

June 3rd, 2014

Several days passed – days and nights spent deepening our connection. It seemed clear to me that the DD process was weaving its magic. I was beginning to understand, not just at an intellectual level, but in a deeply felt and embodied way, how our project might unfold. It was becoming clear that Saritha was 'growing into love' (her words). So whilst our relationship might have been a bit (or perhaps a lot) one-sided at the beginning – with me not just falling, but diving headlong into love and her being cautious and a little anxious about it – that was now changing.

Saritha had already said that the fear she had around moving in with me, that she might feel trapped somehow, had subsided and that indeed, she needn't have worried. She was now feeling happy, relaxed and nurtured in our domesticity. She was deeply enjoying our love nest – the house that I'd designed and built several years earlier. It brings us both the satisfaction of living in a home that is congruent with our values – an ecological dwelling embedded in a spiritual and environmentally conscious community. [1]

---

[1] For more information on the house see
https://findhornblog.wordpress.com/2014/08/04/my-home/

As Saritha moved toward me in love, so I began to feel as seen, valued and loved as I was feeling and expressing toward her. It seemed to me that our love had arrived at some kind of harmony or resonance – an alignment of minds, hearts and souls that had the potential to spiral us into entirely new levels of communion. One particular morning, it was a Monday morning, we never got out of bed. I just knew at an intuitive level that time with Saritha was a greater priority than time in the office. And I was sure that the co-worker and friend with whom I work would support me in that. And sure enough, she did. When I somewhat sheepishly explained my late arrival in the office, she was really happy for me.

That morning in bed was yet another turning point in our deepening. The earnest conversation, the energetic exchange, the sexual exploration, the meeting of minds and hearts was deeply, deeply moving for both of us – but particularly for Saritha I think. She wrote in her journal: 'We cuddle, we kiss, we talk about everything and anything! We talk about our past sexual experiences, we talk about possible future plans. We stay in the present, looking into each other's eyes. So much love and intimacy flowing between us. An overflow of nourishment and contentment.'

Saritha brought us breakfast in bed – superfood muesli we left soaking overnight. We read Rumi to each other – poems I had printed out and blue tacked to the wall above our bed. 'On this lazy morning…' Saritha wrote, '…I found out so much about myself. I purr like a cat when I'm happy. I love loving above anything else and I forget about the rest of life when I'm in these moments of true intimacy. My light and my power get emphasized when I love and I am loved back.' The ecstasy of the morning permeated Saritha's subsequent behaviour. She was so, so loving over the next two or three days. I have never, or at least cannot remember, ever feeling so loved. I was feeling totally blissed out. It felt like some kind of dream and a miracle.

THE WISDOM OF
EARNEST HEMMINGWAY

June 5th, 2014

All men fear death. It's a natural fear that consumes us all. We fear death because we feel that we haven't loved well enough or loved at all, which ultimately are one and the same. However, when you make love with a truly great woman, one that deserves the utmost respect in this world and one that makes you feel truly powerful, that fear of death completely disappears. Because when you are sharing your body and heart with a great woman the world fades away. You two are the only ones in the entire universe. You conquer what most lesser men have never conquered before, you have conquered a great woman's heart, the most vulnerable thing she can offer to another. Death no longer lingers in the mind. Fear no longer clouds your heart. Only passion for living, and for loving, become your sole reality. This is no easy task for it takes insurmountable courage. But remember this, for that moment when you are making love with a woman of true greatness you will feel immortal.

Such is my love for Saritha right now.

DEEPENING THE PROCESS

June 10th, 2014

We proceeded with the DD process. The next phase involved the writing of objectives. This we did by writing our own take on what objectives we thought we should have for the month. Then we compared, collated and distilled them into the following:

OBJECTIVES

1. To co-create the principles and practices by which we live this month.
2. To establish a practice of conscious unconditional love.
3. To courageously disseminate the essence of our project in order to inspire healing, openness and discussion about love, intimacy and sexuality in the community.
4. To pro-actively take our commitment to unconditional love to the world. [1]

_____

[1] My diary, the blog that followed and this book can all be seen as direct outcomes of these last two objectives. Saritha and I tacitly agreed to share transparently, openly and without fear of the consequences, so that others may see that they're not alone in their innermost thoughts and feelings. Knowing we are not alone can be a catalyst for growth, healing and transformation. I have had more than a few people ask me (sceptically, in most cases) what was the motivation for publishing this book? Why on Earth would we want to expose ourselves - our shadows and our needs,

The idea to develop conscious unconditional love had been a latecomer to the process. Surprisingly, it hadn't appeared at all in our Dreaming, although it had crept into our vows. Now it seemed obvious to us both that this was indeed the core objective of this month long project, adventure, experiment, research… call it what you like. Once we'd made this realisation, I retrospectively added it to our inventory of dreams. We were both very aware, and had been all along, of the likely limit to our time together. Saritha was always going to have to leave the UK at the end of June when her visa expired. We're going to meet up again at ZEGG in early July, but after that she is booked to go to Tamera – to the Summer University and the Love School.[1] And I knew that at the Love School, she'd almost certainly be exploring sexually with other men, so the chances of 'losing her' to another were high.

However, to me, her travel plans represented her walking her path, continuing on her journey of discovery and growth into her fullest potential as a change-maker and activist. This indeed, is a huge part of my admiration for her. I so love her drive and commitment to her self-realisation. It's little different from the drive I've had for myself, since I established my values as a teenager. So how can I not support her in that? Besides which, my vow to her of unconditional love, requires me to release her to be who she wishes to be. And of course, it's painful to contemplate.

All the while we were continuing with our practices. We'd established a regular morning routine of yoga, followed by breakfast, drawing cards for the day (Insight, Setback and Angel Cards), followed by Taizé singing and the 8.30am

---

wants, desires and proclivities? Well, this is exactly why. We believe in transparency for the sake of it. The more we humans can fully share with each other what is going on for us, then the greater can be our individual and collective healing and transformation.
[1] ZEGG and Tamera are ecovillages in Germany and Portugal respectively. See www.zegg.de/en/ and www.tamera.org/index.html.

community meditation in the Sanctuary.[1] We didn't stick to it meticulously. Sometimes early morning love-making would take priority and there were other interventions, but on the whole, we were both enjoying the regular practices and benefiting greatly. I was doing yoga for the first time ever and feeling fitter and stronger for it.

My breakfast staple was now muesli, soaked overnight, with fruit, quite different from that of the past six or eight years – hot smoked salmon on toast. For this, my inner critic was truly grateful. I'd been wanting and meaning to give up farmed salmon for some time and never managed to find the motivation. So once again, Saritha coming into my life had offered me an opportunity for transformation; she provided me with the incentive to become vegan – to better align as two souls travelling together, possibly very briefly, into deeper love and intimacy. She had also made changes to her preferred modus operandi. She had forgone, for example, her preference to not eat breakfast before meditating.

We were both greatly enjoying singing and meditating with the community each morning. It was a joy and a privilege to be able to walk across the road and along a narrow winding path to the Nature Sanctuary for Taizé, almost as if it were an extension of our home – a fairy house at the bottom of our garden. And for me, the group meditation in the Main Sanctuary was proving particularly helpful in establishing my nascent practice. All along we were following through with our other intentions: to relate consciously; to spend quality time together; to spend time in nature; and to share our life stories.

We were building a culture of sorts.

---

[1] More information on these practices is available from my blog: www.findhornblog.wordpress.com. See the first few posts in particular.

SAILING

June 13th, 2014

We spent a lovely couple of days sailing with a good friend. It was a joy to get away from work and computers and our busy community life. And it was nourishing to be as close to nature as one is on a yacht. The weather was less than perfect, but that didn't affect our mood – one of quiet, joyous communion, I'd say, with the sea, the landscape, the boat and each other. The winds were near perfect for sailing. We left from Banachro and made good progress to and from Loch Torindon. The seas were kind, the scenery magnificent and the company congenial. Our host was a most affable and laid-back skipper. It was a joy and a privilege to be invited out. Saritha seemed to have a lovely time. It was great to be able to drag her away from her work commitments, to see her slow down and soften. I so enjoyed being able to share the experience with the woman I loved.

PRINCIPLES

June 16th, 2014

To help us stay the course, as a kind of recap of where we'd been and where we were headed with the DD process, we spent an evening creating a *Karabirrdt*. (The word is aboriginal for spider's web). This involved writing on post-it notes the various elements of our Dreaming, Planning, Doing and Celebrating and then locating the notes on a simple grid. We overlaid the grid on a window – the one overlooking the garden and the neighbours beyond, raising their curiosity, as we later learned. We didn't complete the process, but I could see how it was a technically accurate and fun way to represent the whole of the project, almost like a board game.

On the following evening we started another exercise. We were to write down a set of principles for how we were to live life inside the container. Saritha had been keen to do this for a while – she said it was long overdue. But it felt to me like a process too far. Weren't we already living the dream? Enacting the planning? Following the practices? Why did we now need a set of principles to guide us when we seemed to be doing just fine as it was? Saritha suggested that we would need them to guide us once the 'honeymoon' was over. Symptomatically, I hadn't considered that.

We didn't get far with the process; it didn't flow. We

started by naming a series of key concepts, practices and values. Then we each chose the three that we felt were most important. The overlapping keywords, those we both valued, were then woven into the following sentences:

PRINCIPLES:
1. *We share our truth daily and listen empathetically to deepen the intimacy in the relationship.*
2. *We support each other on our individual paths.*

That was as far as we got. I assumed that there needed to be many more principles than these. And for my taste, the first was too wordy and 'try hard.' The second worked better I think, but as mentioned, I wasn't convinced that we needed these. We seemed to be doing very well without them. Anyway, we resolved to return to the exercise.

* * *

We spent a truly exquisite weekend together. Saturday dawned brilliantly with a bright blue cloudless sky, little or no wind and warm temperatures. We decided to go for a run on the beach. Neither of us is very fit so about a kilometre of running was about all we could manage, but it was enough for us to work up a sweat and feel ready to jump into the ocean – the North Sea. For me, it was only the second time I had done so in eight years. The first time was just after I'd fallen in love with my last lover. It seems that new love encourages me to do crazy things. But in fact, the water wasn't so cold. We emerged invigorated and inspired. Saritha posed for some nude photography. She struck a series of stunning yoga poses on the beach with sand, pebbles and dunes as background. I got some excellent pictures, which I printed for her in the days following.

That afternoon we went to bed and stayed there through the evening, night and the following morning. We dived deeper still into intimacy. It was wondrous. One of the most intimate moments involved shaving/trimming each other's pubes – another first for me, and a truly lovely expression of trust and caring. In our conversation we began to broach the issue of next steps. Whilst I had always been clear that I wished for nothing more than the ongoing continuity of our relationship, Saritha had not previously conceded the same. But now, she was beginning to think and talk about coming back to Findhorn after leaving at the end of June, rather than continue on her travels. What joy I felt about this new development and what I felt that it meant i.e. that Saritha was growing more deeply into love. We talked about next steps and future possibilities, including the prospect of getting married so that she could stay in the UK. She seemed open to the idea.

We returned to the writing of principles. This time the exercise flowed much better and resulted in the following:

PRINCIPLES:
We share our truth daily.
We listen empathetically.
We treat each other with kindness and respect.
We support each other on our individual paths.
We regularly monitor whether we still want to be together or not.
We deepen our connection with nature.
We craft our lifestyle with creativity and appreciation.
We practice non-attachment in service to our higher purpose.
We live life to the fullest.

This was better – a concise and powerful list – our very own Common Ground.

We made some runes.

IMPERMANENCE

'Everything is a temporary node in a process of flow'
DD wisdom

June 19th, 2014

Our sexual exploration continues to push new limits.[1] Each time we make love it feels different, fresh and new. Last night, Saritha talked me through a visualisation as we made love, carrying me higher and higher through the chakras to a place of exaltation and ecstasy. Her sexual responsiveness amazes and exhilarates me. It's like nothing I've ever witnessed before. Sometimes she'll climax six or eight times before I do. So beautiful to see, feel and share. I'm experiencing the best sex of my life! What an amazing thing, especially for someone like me with a sexual preoccupation. I'm constantly horny, spending hours of my working day with a semi. And to think that in the last few years I've imagined that my best years, sexually speaking, were behind me – that I might not enjoy another romantic episode, let alone one as

---

[1] Note: There is a deliberate change of tense here. Up to this point, the writing has been in past tense because my diary was started late and compiled retrospectively. However, by June 19th I was up to date and had begun writing in 'real time,' hence the shift into present tense.

29

powerfully erotic as this.

* * *

I looked into Saritha's visa situation and think I have devised a pretty good plan for enabling her to stay in the UK. I'm excited!

* * *

No sooner had I begun to pre-empt the future, to attach to Saritha coming back, than she reminded me of our commitment to staying in the present. Today she posted on Facebook: 'Feeling blissful contentment at the moment. Seeing beauty and love in everything. At the same time, being fully aware that change is the only constant in the Universe and as dark nights pass, so do bright days. Living in the present and being grateful for living in heaven right now.' I was very moved to read of her contentment, of course, but the reference to impermanence was hard to hear, let alone accept.

This morning, after we made exquisite love, did some yoga, shared breakfast then went to Taizé and meditation, Saritha commented that she felt she was living the life she'd dreamed of. Well, if that's the case, I thought, why would she not want to return? She later explained in a text message what she'd meant on Facebook, 'My approach is detachment from the idea that this heavenly feeling should remain forever while enjoying my attachment to you and to this experience right now.' Of course she is right. Things do change. Right now, in this time and place, it feels perfect. We're indeed living in heaven, having the time of our lives. We haven't had any kind of friction let alone an argument. Almost certainly, cracks will show at some point. The 'honeymoon' may well end. The relationship might even deteriorate. It will certainly change, as it has already been doing day-by-day. Nothing is certain.

I love Saritha so much for her wisdom and clarity. I have much to learn from this old soul.

LOVEMAKING

June 20th, 2014

Last night's lovemaking took us to yet another level. I'm beginning to understand how her body works and it's different to most others I have known. Saritha responds much more strongly to slow sex. Most women of my experience have enjoyed strong, even aggressive fucking. But not Saritha. Last night she requested that we go very slowly. She showed me what she meant whilst riding on top of me, then we moved into missionary and finished on our sides. We must have been 'plugged in' for over an hour. The rhythm was glacially slow. And yet, she climaxed two or three times before we finally climaxed together. Throughout, we maintained eye contact, talked and kissed. The union felt total. I cannot describe how blissful it was. For dessert, we followed up with another fuck from behind whilst lying on our sides. Our spooning often goes that way.

Sometimes, indeed often, our orgasms are entirely energetic, involving little or no genital stimulation or contact. We seemed to be able to move into a heightened orgasmic space just through breathing, touching, kissing and feeding off each other's energy – amazing, powerful and wonderful.

* * *

And again, last night – sex and intimacy of a different quality. Saritha is such a great coach, not least of the sexual act. I love how she doesn't hesitate to voice her thoughts about how I could do better, or differently, to improve our sex life. Last night she encouraged me to stop 'ringing the doorbell' (asking or waiting for permission) and instead, enter into and exercise my full masculine power. So I did, and the result was very, very intense. So much so that today we were both feeling a bit shell-shocked I think – I was anyway. And she has been less physical with me than usual.

* * *

We went to Inverness for Saritha to get an eye test and contacts. It was beautiful to see her so happy about the results of the test, which showed no deterioration in the last five years and to see her enjoy 20/20 vision whilst wearing the new contacts – she was like a child at Christmas. We then went to Eden Court for a movie. It was lovely to get off campus and do something together, but equally joyous to come home to our love nest and dream up a delicious late meal of *temaki* with all the (vegan) trimmings. As I write this I'm watching her do the dishes in those beautiful pants she has that show her bum so wondrously. I never imagined I could be so turned on by a woman doing the dishes.

We were just saying how domestic our life has become. We cook, eat, clean, shower and sleep together each day. We're both enjoying it immeasurably. It suits Saritha well – grounds her somehow. She's so much more quietly contented now than she was a few weeks ago. And I'm sure we're enjoying it particularly in the knowledge that it is going to end in a fortnight.

We are packing it in!

* * *

Again, we made a different kind of love last night. The loving was slow and soft and gentle and very, very connected. And then we talked; and then we made love again. This morning I was lying half-awake having had a bad dream (more sad than bad) where I dreamt that my daughter had died. It happened somewhere distant and I was told about it just in passing; I didn't hear any details. My other daughter was with me though. My first thought was of her. I went to her and said, "Oh darling, this must be so sad for you." She looked up at me, kissed me and said, "Yes... don't leave me here. Take me with you." The feeling was of quiet sadness; no more than that. No real grief somehow. I told Saritha about it in a half awake state and wrapped my arms around her in the most intimate of hugs – spooning. I drifted back to sleep and got a clear message – both a feeling and a voice saying that our love was a divine love and it had only one true purpose, which was to radiate out and affect others. I saw and felt our love radiating out into the community and beyond to all beings. I *was* the love and the radiance. I woke and told Saritha. She said, "Welcome home," – a reference, I think, to coming home to God. Hmmm, the bliss, the purity and intimacy of the moment was profound.

After getting up early and writing the above, I went back to bed where Saritha lay dozing. We made love – first energetically, then penetratively. The connection was as close as it has ever been, the rhythm slow. We meditated as we made love and I had my first experience of expanded consciousness since beginning my practice. Saritha talked me through a visualisation as we lay locked together, of penetrating down to the centre of the Earth and then slowly moving upward and outward to the stars. I was transported; I felt as though I was making love with a Goddess. And yes, it felt like coming home – home to my own divinity. Our connection felt total, and so too, my connection with all beings. When we debriefed afterwards, we talked of a universal, transcendent kind of love and how my love for Saritha was a vehicle for connection to the divine. Whilst I had understood previously that this was what we were working toward and had the potential to fulfil, this was the first time I had experienced such total and complete union and connectedness. I felt completely blissful and at peace.

I wondered; where could we possibly go from here? Was there any more deepening to be done? We still had two weeks of our month long project to run. Had we shot our bolt, so to speak?

MORE LOVEMAKING

June 22nd, 2014

The weekend came and went. Our rhythms were a bit misaligned. I had commitments all morning Saturday, Saritha, all afternoon Sunday. But I think we both enjoyed a bit of down time, not least as it enabled us to get on with our separate projects. On Sunday afternoon I got some housework done and mowed the jungle outside – very satisfying.

Sunday night's sex was so different from the spiritually infused lovemaking of previous nights. It was raw, raunchy and base. We started with a slow dance in the living room, which spiralled us into the bedroom where we started with the most exquisite oral sex. I wasn't so hard for some reason so I went down on Saritha and brought her too two orgasms in quick succession. She's such a sexpot. God, how I love her for that. We made love twice more – both powerfully, erotically and physically hot and strong. The second from behind, which ended with Saritha literally screaming into the pillow as we came together. There are no words to describe the feelings.

* * *

Two days later.

Unconditional love is growing. I'm feeling quiet and still within, without anxiety about the present or the future. I think that the previous night's strong expression of my masculinity, last night's sharing with my men's group and also the quiet conversation that Saritha and I are having around her next steps, have had a calming and integrating effect. Last night's sexual expression mirrored my mood. It was slow, infused with sensitivity and so, so loving. I felt waves of unbounded love exiting my heart and enveloping Saritha like a cocoon. I feel that I now love her on a deep, deep level and an infinite scale. At times I feel as though I am love itself.

* * *

The rather serious blister on Saritha's finger burst this morning. She applied a plaster and took the event as a metaphor, as she so often does. "What will happen when our relationship bubble bursts?" she asked. "Will we patch it like we did the blister?" I was caught by surprise, without an answer. Because I'm a romantic and an optimist, the thought had never occurred to me; I just do not think in those terms. I can only imagine our relationship getting better. And I can only see two future scenarios: Saritha will either come back after leaving the country, or she will not. If the former, then we'll pick up where we left off and further deepen our love. If the latter, it will be over and I'll surely grieve deeply. Would I go after her? Not likely; I'm way too committed here at Findhorn. And for better or worse, rightly or wrongly, I'll stand by those commitments.

At lunch time we walked to the beach on a blistering hot day (for North Scotland) – a poignancy filled walk of quiet sharing of possibilities – of different visas that might enable her to stay. Might we get engaged in order to apply for a Fiancée Visa? Get married? I can feel her moving ever closer toward me and the possibility of us staying together. Joy!

* * *

Last night's sex was again, slow, gentle, sensitive and

loving. But then this morning, all hell broke loose! I woke after a really solid night's sleep with a serious hard-on and a very strong desire, not just to fuck, but to possess! So without ceremony or foreplay, let alone permission, I mounted Saritha and forced entry (knowing too, that she was capable of preventing me if she really chose too). I fucked her unmercifully. First from above with her on her side, then from behind. Then for a while with my fingers in both orifices whilst I tongued her clit. She was my sex slave both in my fantasy and in hers. I felt, and she said, that I could do anything I wanted with her. And in the fire of raw desire and selfish gratification I spoke of possessing her – of owning her, exclusively, no matter where in the world she might be in the future – that I would own outright that small but incalculably valuable area of real estate between her legs. I would fence it off and hold exclusive rights to it. And then I fucked her again.

Then we debriefed. We talked of my, now unleashed, shadow – that deepest, darkest part of my subconscious that apparently has laid dormant my whole life – unrecognised, unacknowledged and unseen. We talked of me always wanting to be Mr Nice Guy – to please and to pleasure others, without acknowledging my own needs and wants. I realised that all this fancy talk of unconditional love masks a deeper subconscious desire to possess and own Saritha. I felt enormous gratitude toward this woman, my beloved, who allows and encourages me to dig deep into the layers of my being, to bring the dark into the light, to become whole and more integrated. She is my confidant, my coach, my therapist and my ever-loving partner on this journey into the unknown. She sees the whole of me and she loves me all the more for my complexities and contradictions. I felt so open, vulnerable and liberated from fear. It was yet another moment of profound self-discovery and growth in my understanding of myself.

And then, I fucked her again – this time until I came.

ROAD TRIP

June 24th, 2014

We have just spent three days on the road – on the West Coast, then the North Coast, then Orkney. We hadn't planned to include Orkney, but spontaneously chose to go there as we came toward it – drawn to it, you could say. The highlight of the first day was climbing a picturesque mountain, Stac Polly, north of Ullapool – the first time I have ever climbed a Scottish peak, I'm embarrassed to admit. We didn't make it to the top. Clouds closed in and rain was threatening so we stopped short of the summit, enjoyed a little oral sex-play and a fantasy nude photo-shoot and then headed back down. The walk was relatively easy and the views, spectacular. We were in a great mood, having fun and enjoying being together in nature.

The highlight of the second day involved a long walk to a mighty waterfall through varied micro-climates and eco-systems. The waterfall was truly spectacular – tonnes of water gushing from height into a deep dark pool below. The eroticism of the scene didn't escape us. Very quickly we found a rock ledge perched high above the pool from where we could see the falls. We made love there, slowly, beautifully. We then ventured down to the edge of the pool and stripped off, intending to jump into the dark, cold waters, but thought better of it when we realised that climbing out was going to be very difficult and that anyway, it was a crazy idea. Instead, we did another photo shoot of a naked Saritha holding yoga poses with the waterfall as a backdrop. The walk back to the car was mostly in reverent silence. We were high on nature and each other; the feelings seemed way beyond words.

We drove to Durness for a late lunch on the beach. One of the highlights of the trip was our self-catering. Because of our restricted diet we took a lot of food in a borrowed icebox. Three times we made beautiful lunches of salads and dips followed by delectable, mostly homemade, sweet treats. We spent the second night in a luxury B&B. The bed was enormous and of course we made good use of it, following a beautiful solstice meditation. The day was June 21st and we were as far north as it's possible to go on the UK mainland. We were enjoying the longest possible day to the fullest possible extent.

Next day we set off for Orkney, taking our car across on the ferry. I'd been there before but Saritha had not. Knowing of her affinity with stone circles, I particularly wanted to treat her to one of the most famous in Britain, the *Ring of Brodgar*. We drove past it initially when we saw busloads of tourists there, choosing instead to go to the restored Neolithic village of *Scara Brae*. Saritha was particularly taken by the scale (smallness) of everything. We arrived back at the stone circle to find just a few people there. We took our runes and drew some guidance as we walked around the circle.

Then at one point we ventured into the middle of the circle where we sat opposite each other, did a short meditation, then came together in yab-yum (clothed, of course) for a cuddle and to draw a rune. We drew 'Intimacy.' It was a very poignant moment; the reading was so appropriate, meaningful and encouraging. Here is an excerpt:

The challenge in any intimate relationship involves the balancing of our urge for independence with our desire for union. When strong drives are expressed in positive and healthy ways – in family life, your work in the world, through lovemaking and spiritual practices – you will feel supported both in your going out and your coming in. That is the gift, the mystery of a relationship itself… True intimacy will mark you together even when you are separated and half way round the world. That is the grace of a relationship. That is heaven on Earth.

The reading really opened our hearts and the love between us flowed like a river. The feelings I felt were of complete union with this woman – a fusion of minds, hearts and souls. Oneness! It felt to me like the most intimate moment we'd experienced, and yet there was no sex involved whatsoever – a good lesson for me. Saritha commented that, to her, it felt like a moment spent in an altered reality. I'm not sure that I felt that exactly, but I understood what she meant. What I felt was indeed transcendental, even mystical.

Afterwards we ate lunch in the car. It was raining. The space was confined; it was a bit awkward but we managed well enough and the lunch was, as usual, delicious. We went back via the *Stones of Stennes*, another standing stone circle of lesser size, but with a charm of its own. There was some organised music and storytelling going on, which we listened to for a bit and then headed for the ferry. The non-stop drive home was quiet and mellow. We listened to music and enjoyed the silence at times, feeling comfortable and appreciative of being able to be silent without compulsion to talk. Indeed, throughout the three days, I felt totally comfortable and at ease with Saritha. Travelling with someone can be challenging, but I felt none of that. It was as if we'd done it a hundred times before.

And then, once home, something shifted, radically. I was aware that Saritha had been a touch irritable through the day – a bit snappy. Once home she went into a silent space, with a dark expression on her face. I quizzed her about it to no avail. We showered and went to bed, each of us with our computer, and wrote up our respective diaries. Then we began to process what was going on. The tension lay somewhere between my capacity for making assumptions and sublimating/avoiding and hers for being triggered and feeling irritated. Mine is an old story I've lived with all my life. Hers, I'm just beginning to recognise and to understand.

We processed via some basic constellation work. It was very effective in bringing deep seated emotions to the surface where we could shine a light on them and deal with them. At one point during the role play, we raised the prospect of our relationship being doomed on account of the differences between us. We both felt vulnerable. I got quite emotional. We went back to bed and cuddled, grateful for the effort we'd both put in to dealing with what was our first real emotional challenge – our first 'argument.' I felt very tender and was able to express my vulnerability freely. I felt so grateful for us being able to simultaneously step well outside our comfort zones due to a high level of trust and confidence in each other and in our love.

We then made love like demons.

THE BEGINNING OF THE END… OR
THE END OF THE BEGINNING?

June 25th, 2014

We're now within a few days of Saritha having to leave the country.

Last night we co-created a blog; which we titled *Deepening Intimacy: A project in conscious relationship*. This is in line with our dreaming and planning to document our project and disseminate our findings. It was fun creating it and writing the text for the introductory pages. Saritha has known that I've been diarising our story (although she hasn't yet read it). The idea is to populate our blog with what I have already written, and then continue with regular updates. I'm a little concerned about posting some of my diary – the extracts that are most sexually explicit. However, Saritha seems less concerned. Perhaps we might solicit some feedback from trusted friends before going too public. It's a pity we didn't get this together much earlier, as so much will now need to be posted retrospectively. On the other hand, perhaps we needed to get to the current level of comfort and ease in our relationship in order to be confident enough to do it at all.

The following night, I published my diary on our blog. Saritha was out for the evening at a feedback session with work colleagues. By the time she returned I'd uploaded everything. She sat down to read it, having not done so before, except for one passage that I'd shared with her. So she was reading the blog, both as a participant in its making, but also, as a casual reader might, coming across it for the first time. She read in silence. I wasn't totally sure how she would respond. I was confident that the writing was authentic, but it was my truth, not hers. I was conscious that unless she contributed a lot to the blog, it would end up being a very one-sided account.

When she'd finished reading she went silent with a vacant expression on her face. She said nothing and didn't look at me. She seemed catatonic. I was keen to hear some feedback, but none came. It was a painful moment for me, and for her it seemed. My pain deepened when she went to bed without a word and attempted to sleep. I climbed into bed beside her and held her, but she was unresponsive. After a while I requested we talk. She made an effort, mumbled a few words, which didn't really mean much. She was reluctant to engage, which was more the issue for me. So we slept, me, fitfully.

I was awake at about 4.30, unable to sleep. I woke Saritha and requested that we process. She agreed. We talked – about many things. She said that the blog was beautiful, aside from a few words that she would change. She said it was a love story that deserved to be told. She talked about feeling overwhelmed when reading it. I can certainly understand that. It may well have felt like she was reliving the whole of our time together in the space of the 30 minutes it took to read (Saritha is a speed reader). She talked about the feedback session and how it was also very intense and that she was still processing that experience too.

Saritha felt, so she said, that we were nearing the end of our relationship. I said that I found it hard to accept that something so beautiful had to die. So we talked about life and death (her father's) and the transience of all things – butterflies, mountains, the Earth. We came closer. We made love. It was deep and powerful. But I resolved not to come inside her then, or even at all before she left. Perhaps it would help to detach. If this really must be the end then let it be with grace. We slept a bit more, then woke. We cuddled, meditated on gratitude, then cuddled again and made love some more. It was getting late. I got up, showered and prepared breakfast along with our cards. She eventually joined me, but didn't eat. She looked sullen and irritated, but also open.

What a complex woman is my beloved.

PARTING

June 26th, 2014 (three days before Saritha leaves).

Yesterday was a rough day. Following our challenging night and fractious parting, we had little contact – exchanging just a couple of text messages. We didn't connect at mealtimes in the CC, nor at a community meeting we both attended. Then she had a late meeting to attend. So it was 11pm before we reconnected. Throughout the day I intuited a desire in her to withdraw. In me, I first felt a welling of grief and then a toughening of my resolve. I reasoned that we both have work to do in order to detach. Paradoxically, I think we can do that more gracefully if we do it together rather than separately. It seems paramount that we stay in communication and follow through with our agreed principles, particularly these ones:

We share our truth daily.
We listen empathetically.
We treat each other with kindness and respect.
We support each other on our individual paths.
We regularly monitor whether we still want to be together or not.

If we can do all that, then I'm sure we will navigate closure with grace. Indeed, now that I think about it, it seems that these five principles crystallised exactly for the purpose of guiding us through this final week of closure (and also the week in ZEGG). I continue to be amazed by the wisdom of our DD inspired process and the power of the various 'deliverables' (vows, objectives, principles etc.). I'm beginning to see what John Croft, the originator of Dragon Dreaming, is talking about when he says that DD is fundamentally, 'unconditional love in action.' If we remain in conscious relationship and apply these principles, I'm sure we can love and leave each other unconditionally.

We went to bed around midnight and after some time, reconnected softly and lovingly. We held a check-in[1] and talked through our respective days – the activities and feelings. And with this clarity and empathy, we came close once more. We made love with joy. I couldn't help but be in wonder at the synergy and synchronicity of our lovemaking – waves of energy rising and falling in unison. We woke early, I think because my arms had been wrapped so tightly around her they were completely numb. We made love once more, gently, softly. We rose with plenty of time for our practices: yoga, breakfast, cards and an extended Taizé session. We left home for our respective offices after a sweet, sexy, loving clinch in the porch, in stark contrast to our parting the day before. I wrote on our blog, 'Feeling gratitude for life right now and deep, deep love for Saritha'.

The likelihood of Saritha returning to Findhorn instead of

---

[1] Our check-ins were a device we regularly used to maintain transparency – an essential feature of the consciousness that we sought for our relationship. Whenever either of us felt there were unresolved issues that needed addressing, we wouldn't hesitate to request a check-in, immediately or at the earliest convenient time. A check-in would usually start with a short meditation then whoever made the request would speak their mind whilst the other listened, just listened, without preconception or interruption, ideally with empathy and an open mind. That person would then have time to respond and be received similarly. And so we would alternate until we both felt the issue was addressed and we had reached an understanding. Occasionally, we would hold a check-in to simply share our activities of the day. At other times we would do both.

continuing on her travels is now high. And yet neither of us is assuming that our relationship will be resumed. We're determined to stay in the present and not anticipate the future. Besides, I have a hunch that out time in ZEGG is going to test us, not least because our month-long project will effectively end with her parting. The container that has supported our relationship so effectively will possibly fade, or even crumble.

COMPLETION

June 29th, 2014

It's Sunday evening. Saritha has flown. It's been several days since I posted the last entry – days so intense I was left with no time for writing. We've been attending a three-day workshop entitled 'Love, Sex and Intimacy.' For some weeks, we had seen participation in the workshop as a fitting end to our journey together. And indeed it was, albeit less intensely than I would have liked. Thirty plus participants made for a less intimate workshop than if there had been say, 20, but in fact, the trust and openness that we developed within a very short time catalysed some deep and courageous sharing during the second and third days.

Saritha and I held a parallel workshop of our own in our last week together. It was very intense: lots of processing; some deep sharing; expressions of grief and sadness; much appreciation and celebration; and exchanges of boundless love. Our sex life slowed and quietened somewhat. I think the level of intensity was already such that we had little emotional capacity for the passion that had characterised the previous weeks. On our last night however, we ventured into the sand dunes and after a beautiful walk on the beach, created a sweet love nest for ourselves atop a dune where we made love for the last time, surrounded by lush grasses, purple flowering heather, the sound of the ocean and a vast sky overhead. We felt fully connected to each other and to nature; almost as if we were making love with the vegetation, the ocean, the sky and the Earth itself. It was a divine moment and a glorious way to culminate our sexual journey.

* * *

So what now? Well, Saritha has decided to return to Findhorn, in part I believe, but not entirely, because of our relationship. She's attracted to the idea of deepening her relationship with the Findhorn Foundation so has booked into Experience Week, our introductory programme, at the end of July. This is much sooner than I'd previously imagined, so of course, I'm delighted. She'll forego her planned visit to Tamera and the Love School, I'm relieved to say. But at the same time, I'm not assuming anything apropos the continuity of our relationship. Saritha has made it clear that she values her independence and freedom – an impulse she has ferociously held since a teenager. She carries a fear of being attached, which in her mind I think, equates to being trapped. That is her stuff to deal with; there is little I can do to dissuade her, other than offer her my love and compassion. And of course, I hope that love prevails over fear. I'm reminded of that Leunig poem, *Love and Fear*.

Love and Fear / *Michael Leunig*
There are only two feelings, Love and fear:
There are only two languages, Love and fear:
There are only two activities, Love and fear:
There are only two motives, two procedures,
two frameworks, two results, Love and fear,
Love and fear.

In a week we meet up again at ZEGG – that most marvellous of communities near Berlin. I visited there several times between nine and 13 years ago and loved the place, the people and the culture, so much that I believe I'd be living there now if I could speak German. So it will be great to return to see old friends and soak up the erotically charged atmosphere that pervades there.[1]

Saritha and I talked through our agreements for the week. We decided that we needn't agree one way or the other whether to be open or exclusive sexually. Rather, we vowed to maintain our already established practices: staying in communication and treating each other with kindness and respect. That basically translates into staying connected and checking in with each other before doing anything too precipitous with another.

So we'll see. I'm feeling open and at peace with whatever wants to unfold. Saritha and I have established a rare and beautiful love for each other and I'm confident that our love will guide us into and through the next chapter(s) of our story.

---

[1] For those unfamiliar with the quite radical cultural norms at ZEGG, they include what they call 'liberated love'. It's a version of 'free love' (born of the radical climate of the late sixties) whereby two people who feel physical attraction are encouraged to act upon it – to be open and honest with their feelings and desires rather than resist or suppress them, even if they already have another lover or partner.

SEPARATION

July 3rd, 2014

Today things went awry. I've been sending Saritha daily emails with a bit of news, perhaps a poem, and a photo of the cards I'd drawn for her. Nothing much has come back which I'd put down to her having limited or no internet access. But today I got a one word email from her – 'Congratulations,' in response to my telling her of the birth of my grandchild. That was it! Just one word. So I shot back, 'So how are you going? Feeling better? (I knew she'd been feeling unwell). Anything to say? Love from me as always.' She replied, 'Thank you for the poem and for thinking of me. I've been extra busy! Feeling very distant from you. It seems our month together was a long, long time ago. I wonder how it will be to see you again at ZEGG. xx N.'

I was flabbergasted. How can someone change so quickly for no apparent reason? Such inconsistency is very hard for me to fathom – quite the antithesis of the way (rightly or wrongly) I seek to be in the world, which is to be reliable, dependable, consistent. I felt feelings of dismay, confusion and unusually for me, anger. 'Is she really trying to sabotage our beautiful relationship?' I asked myself. 'How is that possible? How can she possibly be so self-absorbed? It makes no sense!' But, for better or worse, I kept my cool. 'After all...' I thought '... it may just be a temporary malaise, and once we meet again, we'll reconnect (like we did after Brighton).' So I shot back, 'Goodness me. Such a change in you is hard to comprehend. Can you fathom it yourself?' to which she responded, 'Well, it's pretty normal for me to feel disconnected when I'm far away. You've seen how I am with my family.' This is true; she was disconnected from me whilst in Brighton and she's generally quite disconnected from her family in Canada. I wrote back, 'Yes indeed. So you're the exception to the rule that absence makes the heart grow fonder. Colder, in your case, perhaps. All I feel I can do is hold you in my heart and wish you well. Take care sweetheart. G xx.'

I was being my usual calm and considerate self – trying to be understanding, compassionate and loving, but in doing so, not being true to myself. I felt empty saying it. Sometimes I really wish I wasn't so damned loving. I actually felt quite angry, but I also felt that this wasn't a discussion to be had in two or three line emails. So I swept my anger aside. Afterwards, as time passed I got more and more pissed off. I thought, if she'd deliberately wanted to alienate and push me away, she could not have done a much better job of it. Was she really going to pull the plug? Or is she just playing games, being manipulative, being an arsehole? 'Why the hell did I call her sweetheart?' I wondered. And then I'd feel guilty for thinking so badly of her. Perhaps She's just feeling low, expressing her truth and without any agenda. I can imagine that's possible. But I'm no longer confident that I know, or can know. I don't feel enough of a connection with her to be able to tell intuitively. I feel I've lost trust.

I think I started to loose trust a couple of days after she left saying she was intending to do a lot of writing on our blog whilst at the airport overnight and in the near future. She didn't post a thing. Or then, a couple of days later, the first time I hear from her, she sent a one line email explaining that Internet access was challenging where she was and that she was using what access she had to work. Why would she tell me that she was prioritising work over our relationship if she didn't intend to hurt and push me away? So this afternoon I thought, really, this woman is just too 'high maintenance' for me. Because I'm so sensitive, it makes no sense to be with a woman who appears so uncaring. It's just too hard. So I decided, not for the first time, to completely release any thoughts of us getting back together, whether at ZEGG or subsequently. And as soon as I'd done so, I felt better.

I decided to book my flight to Australia at Xmas. I'd been holding off doing so because of the possibility of Saritha coming with me, and perhaps me going with her to Canada on the same round trip, but I can see that if there is any small chance of that at all, she's not going to commit to it for quite some time. There are some very cheap deals going right now that will not last long and the later I book of course, the more expensive it will get. I'm usually booked for such a trip well before now. So I'll do that tomorrow. Conceivably she could still join me there, but if I book a return flight, there is little chance I'll go to Canada with her. It feels good to have made that decision. Since my daughter gave birth recently, I've been feeling a very strong urge to book this flight. I feel I have to follow that particular pull on my heart right now.

So that's it. I'm looking forward to seeing Saritha at ZEGG, if only so that we can get some clarity, because we'll need to if I'm to continue with this relationship. I don't want to put up with this shit anymore. Now I think I'll go and pull down the Rumi poetry from above the bed. I've been waiting for some clarity around that and I think it has just landed. I'm going to post this on the blog where Saritha might read it, or not. She may not be at all interested in my posts. I just don't know anymore. But we do have an agreement to speak our truth, so that's reason enough to post. Whether she reads it or not, and if so, how she receives it, will be telling.

EPIPHANY

Through the eyes of love you are perfect
Through the eyes of love you are free
Through the eyes of love you are innocent
I am you and you are me

July 5th, 2014

Sitting in transit at Schiphol airport, I'm listening to the above song by the Findhorn Singers. On the flight over from Aberdeen I had a series of breakthrough realisations such that now I'm feeling completely embarrassed by my last blog post (the previous chapter) entitled *Separation*. But I won't withdraw it. I'll leave it there as a memo to myself – to be more conscious of my edges and my lurking shadow. It's so clear to me now what transpired when I expressed those feelings of anger, disappointment and distrust yesterday. It was my underlying, subconscious insecurities. The loss of trust I felt had little to do with Saritha or her actions or failure to act, although it certainly felt like that at the time. The loss of trust I felt was entirely within me; it was a loss of trust in my core self. My response was solely due to my getting lost in my own needs and wants – in particular, my need to be loved. In the process, I lost sight of our interconnectedness, Saritha and I, our oneness. I lost sight of the understanding that I reach from time-to-time (and obviously lose from time-to-time), that she is perfect, she is free and she is innocent.

So it seems that unconditional love is not a constant, not a static state that one attains in relation to another from which there is no going back. I know the feeling of unconditional love. I've known unconditional love for Saritha in moments and for periods in the last few weeks. It bubbles up when I'm fully centred and aligned. It absconds when I lose touch with my core self. And I also know that such love in still growing in me; the instances and periods of stillness, acceptance, true understanding and compassion are landing more frequently and for longer. It's a process. It doesn't come easy. It takes effort and consciousness.

I'm about to board the flight to Berlin. I'm feeling deep gratitude right now, for the presence of Saritha in my life and the resultant learning and personal growth that the relationship brings. (I seem to recall saying that before). I resolve to do my absolute best to remain in that space of gratitude during our time in ZEGG – gratitude for her being who she is, for her presence in my life, and for all that is. I resolve to remain conscious and open-hearted. There's a strong likelihood that the unconditional nature of my love for Saritha will be tested at ZEGG. We'll be immersed in a culture of radical liberated love. Sometimes (at parties and dances) we'll find ourselves in an atmosphere infused with eroticism. She'll be engaging with other men, perhaps flirting, perhaps kissing, perhaps going further. This will no doubt test my resolve, but I feel I'm up for the challenge and look forward to the continued growth and learning that it will bring.

RECONNECTION 2

July 7th, 2014

   As expected, our reconnecting has not been easy. Saritha arrived at lunch time. I saw her from a distance, outside the dining hall as I came down from the Internet Café. She was greeting and hugging old friends in her usual delightful way and I could see that she was aware of me coming closer. I felt awkward. I wanted to wrap my arms around her and lift her to me, but I intuited that she was feeling resistant, unsure and distant. She smiled and we hugged, but it was not the hug I sought. It was perfunctory and short. She pulled away to engage more with others. It was hard. I felt hurt.

   We didn't connect at lunch. Saritha wanted to sit with others. That too was hard, but I reasoned that she was needing space and expressing her independence. Fair enough, I suppose. But I decided that we needed to talk, to check-in. So after lunch I requested we do that and she agreed. We went to my room and spent a couple of hours reconnecting. We sat in silence for a short while then checked in. Saritha shared her feelings of disconnection. She mentioned that at the moment of meeting outside the dining hall, she had indeed felt resistant. She felt that I was laying claim to her somehow. And she hadn't wanted to be seen as one of a couple. This was hard to hear. At the time I was feeling nothing of the sort, but rather, just the very same deep love I've had for her all along. But obviously my body language or something else was communicating differently. And behind her fears, I'm pretty sure, are the childhood rooted issues that give rise to her compulsive need for independence that I've written about already. I imagine that my compulsive needs and wants (for love and connection) similarly originate in early childhood experience.

After my response, we went into silence for a while, then lay down on the bed. We talked more, sharing about our week. She told of having spent the night with a guy in Berlin, without having sex. I wasn't surprised to hear it. I'd intuited as much. And we talked about her changeability compared with my constancy. She conceded that she was chameleon-like, soaking up the qualities of the current environment she is in and leaving behind the one she has come from. She explained that in the week of the DD gathering, she was so immersed in the intensity of it that she lost contact with me, which was the message I'd been getting, but it was good to hear her explanation.

After a while Saritha brightened up. The chatting was bringing us closer and rekindling some of the lost tenderness. She offered to tell me about her week in detail. It was fascinating – such an intense week, culminating in a very deeply effective shamanic sweat lodge. I was envious, I must say. I would have loved the experience. And she said she offered an open space, sharing about our project, which she presented to three people, including John Croft. She got positive feedback, she said, so we decided to hold a similar sharing at the conference later in the week. This could be a forerunner of the workshop we'd dreamed of giving at some point in the future.

Anyway, I shared about my week – the birth of my grandchild and the feelings that had come up when she sent those one line emails and the one about her sense of disconnection. Saritha was impressed that I had gotten angry. It's not an emotion that I often allow in myself. It was good to be able to share about it and to receive feedback. We came closer and spent a short while cuddling (not very successfully however – I was too keen and overstepped her boundaries). We talked some more and reached a place of understanding. I stroked her for a while, which I appreciated for the opportunity to express my caring and she appreciated for the peace that she was able to access. She was tired, needing sleep. But she had things to do – to register and check in with others. So she went. I felt a whole lot more resolved and at peace.

And we'll see what happens next.

WHAT HAPPENED NEXT

July 7th, 2014

What happened next was more processing. We met again in my room that evening, by accident actually. She was there to repack the suitcases (we swapped small and large suitcase due to the different weight limitations on our respective flights). When she finished, we lay on the bed and processed some more. This is one thing I think we're very good at – honest, open talking about what's going on for us, being transparent and gaining clarity. We identified a push-pull dynamic that has been with us for a while; when I become needy, she withdraws. Furthermore, she attempts to sabotage or undermine my actions. We talked about my vulnerability and her 'dragon' – the anger that arises in her when she perceives me as being weak. Then we conducted an exercise we'd done in the workshop, *Love Sex and Intimacy*, mirroring aspects of the other that we struggle with the most. I role-played her anger, resentment and irritation and she reflected my lack of self-confidence, as she sees it. It was edgy and healthy and brought more understanding to each of us.

It's been a very intense day, but a good one. We've achieved a lot. I'm feeling heard and seen and I think she is too. I'm relaxed and at peace. (Yes, I know I've said that before). I learn more about myself every single day and that is an amazing and wonderful thing. She's gone off to her tent now. She's camping with Canadian friends, which she's very happy about. And I'm happy for her. She deserves some nurturing from those lovely women.

THE LAST POST
(FOR A WHILE, ANYWAY)

July 8th, 2014

I've woken this morning in a totally different kind of space. I don't know whether it was all the processing we did yesterday and the subsequent realisations and learning, or whether it was simply the exercise we did late last night – in semi-darkness as the daylight entering the room faded. But today I feel like a different person; I'm fully in my power. Looking back, I can see that this started late last night. On the way back to my room after posting *What Happened Next*, I heard music coming from the San Diego Café – the party venue. So I dropped off my computer and headed down. The most fabulous party was in full swing and I was really in the mood to dance! I had a great time, moving with gusto, interacting with several of my female friends, flirting a bit and having fun. Then I had a lovely long chat with one of them, a couple of drinks and eventually headed for bed, invigorated and nourished.

This morning I've woken raring to go. I've decided to throw myself into the conference as both participant and support person. I'm determined not to lose any more of my time here in processing with Sara – that is what I'll call her in this post anyway. Saritha is her spiritual name and it is the one

I've been using to date as it represents that side of her that I most appreciate and honour – her commitment to her spiritual path, her purpose and her journey in the world. On the other hand, Sara, her given name, to my mind represents her worldly persona – the part that harbours her shadow: the critic, the witch, the bitch and the drama queen.

Sara is undoubtedly a complex and layered woman, that much is clear. She can be wondrous, but she is also moody, changeable, unpredictable and volatile – immature in that sense, I would say if I was being particularly judgmental. I now realise that when I am in that state she identified in the exercise we did as lacking in self-confidence, I trigger in her that aspect which I role-played, which is her anger, her irritation and her resentment. This is really the dynamic at work, the one which I described in the last chapter as push-pull. I think it is actually more like withdrawal/flight versus anger/resentment, the same dynamic that triggered our first 'argument.' Well, I've really had enough of it. I realise just how much of a vicious cycle it is; it spirals out of control, or at least it could do if we were not in communication, conscious and processing. So I've decided that I don't need it in my life right now. It's unhealthy for both of us, individually and for our relationship. Anyway, I wonder whether it's really self-confidence that I've lost (given that I've felt very self-confident all my life) or confidence in her. I mean, for fucks sake, wouldn't most people step right back into a relationship as wonderful as ours has been. Why all this drama?

It somewhat reminds me of my relationship with my ex-wife who regularly criticised me. Often for her, I wasn't a good enough husband or father when in fact, I think I did pretty damned well at both. But sadly, I had little of the understanding of myself back then that I have developed through being with Sara. I was never able to learn and grow in the same way and that was when my predisposition for flight over fight was firmly established. Yesterday's interaction felt at times like a rerun of aspects of my marriage, except that this time we processed. However, I felt all the same condemnation coming from Sara that I used to cop from my ex, the essential judgment being that I'm not good enough. The processing we did around it has had two outcomes. I've now recognised the dynamic for what it is, and my role in it. And furthermore, I've decided that I don't need the relationship, at least not this version of it, in my life right now. If she fundamentally believes that I'm not good enough then I think the relationship really is (and was always) doomed.

So I'm going to get on with having an excellent conference; throw myself into it, contribute lots and learn what I can. I expect to be 'in the flow' (as I know I am on these adrenalin fuelled occasions), gregarious, pro-active and 'out there.' I feel no desire to spend time with Sara the drama queen or, for that matter, any great desire to even be with Saritha the goddess. For the rest of the week, the relationship is, at best, on hold. If it never revives then that will be that – the natural cycle of birth and death, beginnings and endings. I'll take a break now from journaling and posting. This week is going to be intense. I intend to live it to the full and not be on my computer. I'll resume posting next week.

PUSHING OUR EDGES:
AN EXPERIMENT IN 'LIBERATED LOVE'

July 10ᵗʰ, 2014

Saritha and I reconnected within a day of my last post (the previous chapter). She had read it and was deeply hurt; she was in the depths of despair. I had expected the post, indeed, much of my last four or five posts, to elicit a strong response, but I didn't anticipate such sadness and hurt. I guess I'd expected something more like anger and irritation. I was saddened myself to see and feel her pain. I commented that the pain felt as deep and as low as the beauty and exhilaration of our relationship had been high back in June. When we'd talked and processed enough to enable some softening and reconnection, she told me that a man with whom she had bonded during a course at Findhorn some nine months earlier was here for the conference. She'd previously told me of their relationship. They'd been together, but not fully sexually active, because she'd felt that they didn't have time enough and she declined to go there recklessly. Anyway, they'd met earlier in the day and she felt the same attraction that she had previously. Furthermore, she was interested in exploring this attraction with him in the coming days. She said there was 'unfinished business' between them – the implication being that she wanted to engage with him intimately, perhaps sexually.

I was taken aback; my chest tightened and my heart was racing. I've had open relationships before, several over many years, but never have they been with someone I was living with or who was even in the vicinity. My open relationships have been long distance affairs with women in other countries and they made sense to me in that context. Sharing a lover with another man in real-time and space was altogether another matter. Saritha talked of the tension she was feeling between being in relationship with me and her desire and need for freedom. She felt inhibited, shackled. This made me sad. Limiting her freedom in order that she be with me is totally unacceptable and is the opposite of what I'd want for any partner at any time – which would be that she grow, develop and become who she most passionately sought to be in the world. I'd hope that she would 'follow her bliss' to quote Joseph Campbell.

I was forced to look deeply into my heart for a response. I felt many emotions, including fear – specifically the fear that I might lose her. But I reasoned that I simply had to agree to her request for freedom to explore with this guy. How could I not if I truly loved her and wanted her to feel free. So I agreed, apprehensively. What better place to attempt such an experiment than at ZEGG where there is already an ethos of, and a lot of community support for, the practice of 'liberated love.' In any case, I said, we needed to make *some* agreements around how we would be together, because currently we had none; we'd not been feeling close enough for long enough, since arriving, to have created such a container.

Saritha was so happy. She sat up, moved closer and nestled in alongside me. I grabbed the computer and we started writing the following set of agreements.

1. *That we maintain our commitment to being in a conscious relationship i.e. we recommit to our partnership.*
2. *That we bring ZEGG-based experience, wisdom and values to our relationship and that:*

65

- *During the week we agree to remain in partnership, but also be free to be with others.*
- *We agree that communication is crucial. We will hold check-ins daily, in the evenings, either after dinner or at 10pm.*
- *We will consciously tap into the wisdom available at the conference... in Forum,[1] workshops and conversations, etc.*
- *We will approach the week as a research project and experiment, the object of our investigation being:*
  - *Possibilities for combining partnership and freedom.*
  - *Issues and feelings of possession, ownership and jealousy.*
- *The methods we will employ during this research will include:*
  - *Sharing with each other the emotions that arise throughout the week.*
  - *Using the available support (of friends, home groups, Forums, etc.).*
  - *Telling our story (of this experiment) at appropriate venues. (There will be several opportunities for this in the conference programme – workshops, home groups, etc.).*

I was much happier with the idea after we'd drawn up this 'charter.' It felt confirming of our being primary partners, such that this new experiment would probably not threaten our connection. In subsequent conversations I became surer of her love and commitment to our relationship and that made all the difference. We were now both quite excited by this prospect. It seemed as if we'd launched a new phase in our project in conscious relationship, which had not had much direction since the end of June. I looked forward to the challenge – to the test of my strength and resolve.

We then made love, making good use of the iron-framed bed and some scarves. For me, it was some of the most powerful and erotic lovemaking we had experienced. It was completely mind-blowing.

---

[1] Forum is a communication tool developed at ZEGG. It is used to ensure transparency, particularly in matters of love, sex and intimacy.

AN APPROPRIATE TITLE ESCAPES ME

July 11th, 2014

Last night, Saritha left me to be with another man – the man she'd been with during the course at Findhorn, the one with whom she had great, but non-penetrative sex, much as we had had before she went to Brighton. She was dressed beautifully in the sarong I'd given her, without knickers. It was the very same outfit she'd worn for our ritual, the one which preceded me entering her for the first time. The symbolism could not have been clearer – she was preparing to make love with this man.

The day had already been very challenging. I discovered a jealous streak in me I really didn't know I had. (Previously, I'd lived my whole life believing I didn't have a jealous bone in my body.) During the morning, my monkey brain played all kinds of tricks as I struggled with the pain of fear, self-doubt, separation and jealousy. During lunch, I noticed Saritha talking for extended periods with two good-looking, mature and charismatic guys – just the kind of men she fancies. My 'monkey mind' was convinced she was flirting with a view to scoring. I spent the afternoon working hard to dispel the voices and regain my peace of mind; and I largely succeeded. I spent time in contemplation – recalling and reviewing the principles behind our new agreements. Namely, that Saritha is a free and autonomous human being on her own path. That she's entirely independent of me and I have no claim on her. Indeed, my deep love for her behoves me to fully support her journey of growth and self-discovery. And in any case, I know her to be a determined seeker of her truth and that my resistance or even my being in pain was not going to deflect her from that. I also benefited from a lot of community and personal support – authentic human contact with friends, an inspiring workshop on free love and a Forum session, all of which enabled me to find some stillness by the end of the afternoon.

I met Saritha for a check-in over dinner. Then we sat with her other lover for a while and established some considerable clarity and understanding – discussing how we might enact our particular *ménage a trois* with love, trust and transparency. After dinner, she and I went to my room to process further. I was grateful for all of these opportunities. They made a huge difference to my thinking and feeling. It was clear that our single most important principle i.e. to stay in communication, was working to bring clarity and stillness. So by the time she left me to meet him, I felt able to bless her on her way. At least, my head was able. My heart was thumping like crazy.

I went to the pub and had heartfelt chats with some very good friends from Findhorn. Sharing my situation with them really helped. And I chatted with Alisa, the woman who had co-presented the workshop on free love that had so inspired me earlier in the day. She listened to my story with interest and presence. She had several pearls of wisdom to offer, not least, that 'there is nothing less sexy than a man who is clingy.' God, how I know this already; yet it was good to be reminded. When I talked about my feelings of loss (loss of my lover, loss of the relationship, loss of potential) Alisa said that the loss I felt, the missing part, was in me. The work I had to do, she advised, was to restore that absent piece of me that would enable me to feel whole.

I went to be bed after midnight, felt reasonably at peace and slept ok. I woke to write this post at 5am then, with

Alisa's advice in mind, went to the early morning meditation. It didn't work for me – people were coming and going; I was distracted. I look forward to meeting Saritha soon at breakfast or later this morning. I hope to find her feeling happy and fulfilled.

AFTERMATH

July 13th, 2014

As I write this post, Saritha is lying asleep beside me. She's exhausted. Her busy work life, drama filled love life and the intensity of interaction generally pervading the conference have taken their toll.

Today could not have been more different to yesterday in terms of my own personal experience. Saritha and I held a check-in after breakfast. She told me of her evening – of how she'd not had sex with her other lover, although they had made love, and that she'd stayed with him overnight. They had mostly talked. Furthermore, she had not forgotten me, had been concerned about my wellbeing and actually looked for me in the pub at around one in the morning, an hour or so after I had gone to bed. I was touched by all of this. She seemed enriched and fulfilled by the time spent with her friend. I sensed she'd followed her heart to the limit of its desire, although I'm not entirely sure. It's possible that she was holding back for fear of hurting me and that thought made me sad. What would be the point of us conducting such an experiment in 'liberated love' if she did it only half-heartedly? I then shared about my activities of the previous evening and the shell shock I felt upon waking. I was numb and without feeling, I told her, the extreme emotion of the previous day had left me drained and empty.

Soon after our check-in, I met with Saritha's other lover to talk. We had a beautiful heartfelt exchange, telling of our experiences in love, interests and passions in life, and some of our life stories. We were getting to know each other; it felt as though I was making a new friend. I liked him very much and actually, that made a positive difference to how I felt about him being with Saritha. I spent the rest of the day in the same daze that I felt upon waking – a kind of numbness of the mind and heart, which was a relief in a way following the intensity of the previous day.

I thought Saritha would spend more nights with him, but in the evening she came to my room for our regular check-in and told me she had no such plan for the evening. Furthermore, her friend was leaving in the morning. We shared about our respective days and she quickly fell asleep (at about 8pm). We both slept deeply for eight or nine hours.

BREAK-UP

July 15th, 2014

I'm sitting in Tegel Airport, Berlin an hour early, partly because of my aversion to running late (so leaving plenty of time to spare) and partly because of the brilliance of the German transportation system. I took two buses and a train to get here; each connection was seamless. The journey took two hours at a cost of something like £10. Amazing! I'm listening to Art Pepper on my new Bluetooth operated headphones that relay wirelessly to and from my phone, eating a yummy ciabatta and feeling pretty good about myself and about life in general, despite an emotional farewell and departure this morning.

I left Saritha in bed, after we'd spent an hour sharing (me) and counselling (her). The last couple of days since my last post have been somewhat of a blur. I'm struggling to compile the narrative, which usually flows so easily to the keyboard. But the upshot is that we (well, me actually) have decided that it's just too hard to consider our relationship a partnership and that I'd much rather think of it as a no-strings-attached friendship. Saritha's primary partnership is with God. It's hard to compete with that! Nor would I want to; the thing I most admire about her (as I've said before) is her commitment to her spiritual journey.

However, in her mind, this means being open to whatever wants to unfold – being in the flow and open to possibility (which, of course, includes remaining open to being with other men. Indeed this is the nub of her approach to relationships.) To my mind, however, it simply means an inability to commit. And this, I find extremely challenging. We have talked at length, for example, about her coming back to Findhorn and getting more deeply involved. And indeed, she is booked into a programme starting at the end of next week. We have also talked about her coming back for the second workshop on *Love, Sex and Intimacy*, which starts on the same weekend (so she can't do both). Both of these scenarios are real possibilities, but neither is certain. She hasn't yet done what she needs to in order to make them happen: to write a letter of application for the course; book a flight back; or, book the workshop (although I'll probably do that on her behalf if the fee is refundable).

Indeed, just yesterday she was still unsure whether she'd be going to Spain on the flight tomorrow that she has already booked. The DD workshop that she was intending to facilitate in Andalusia has been cancelled due to a lack of participants, symptomatically I believe, because she and her co-facilitator didn't allow enough time for promotion. She probably will go because she doesn't want to forego the cost of the ticket. What happens when she gets there is literally in God's hands, as is whether, or not, she will feel the call to return to Scotland within the next week.

Added to this is the unhealthy dynamic that arises between us when we're separated. Saritha loses the connection we have whilst I deeply miss her and crave communication, even if it's just an occasional brief email or text message with some news or a few words of affection. But such acknowledgement of our connection seldom comes when she's travelling. She feels lost to me. I see this as a manifestation of our differences at an archetypal level; that Saritha is strongly the Warrior whilst I am equally strongly the Lover, but perhaps that's material for another post.

I have also really struggled with what I see as Saritha's lack of constancy. At ZEGG she generally didn't want us to be perceived as a couple whilst in public; she insisted on being demonstrative of her independence. This was quite the opposite of how we were back in Findhorn, which was to be demonstrative about our love and affection for one another. The latter is my natural way of being with someone I love. The former may well be hers, but I found it too contrived, counter-intuitive and weird; I really struggled with it.

I'm also tired of her manising (a new word freely adapted from womanising). At ZEGG she would tell me of her interest in particular men and the flirting she did with them. She would say, I imagine, that by telling me this she was just being transparent, as we had agreed. But I'm really not sure how much of such talk is based in reality and how much is self-obsession, fantasy and/or thought experiment. Or, how much of it is she doing in order to assert and remind me of her independence? So I find myself asking, is she being deliberately manipulative? Further, she must know that such talk is hurtful. I wonder, does she not care? Or worse, is she being deliberately hurtful?

I know that hopes and expectations can be unproductive and being attached to future events is problematic. For that matter, being attached in any way is fraught. Buddhism has got it right; the only really important journey in life is the one taken with oneself and it's all about finding non-attachment. So that's what I'm seeking now – detachment from aspirations I had for our relationship and also from Saritha, herself. It will help make sense of this soup of experiences, thoughts and emotions that have been my inner life of the last three months. It will also help me deal with the day-to-day, moment-to-moment, interpersonal dynamics between us. The truth is, *my* truth is, that I'm tired of dealing with the required high level of maintenance seemingly inherent in our relationship – the amount of processing that it requires. I'm tired of the push-pull dynamics and bluntly, I'm tired of her behaviour.

So I feel that our relationship is effectively over. And I'm ok with it. In this moment it feels like a relief. I think it's tragic mind you. We had such a good thing going for the middle month of the three we spent together. Looking back, we spent the first month in preparation for the second – a brilliant, spectacular, shining jewel of a month (the one based on our project), which was followed by a third month of entropy and slow break-up. It seems we failed to hold it together without the support of the container. That's telling, I think. It casts further doubt on our essential compatibility. Perhaps I'm just too sensitive and open-hearted to be with a woman like Sara a.k.a. Saritha.

If she returns to my community and we do decide to try again, then it's going to have to be within the context of another very carefully designed container. With the benefit of all this experience to now draw on, I can imagine we might feasibly negotiate a more grounded set of intentions, objectives, principles and practices to take us forward into the next phase, or the next project. We could conceivably come out of this even stronger and our relationship be even more conscious, but it's going to need will – her will and my will. And I'm not sure that either of us is feeling very willing right now.

ON ARCHETYPES

July 18th, 2014

I raised the matter of archetypes in the previous chapter. I want to explore that theme a little more here, hoping that it might help us understand some of the dynamics of our relationship. If it rings true, it might explain some of the tension between us. And such insights could help ease the sense of loss I will feel should we agree to fully separate, or alternatively, illuminate a way for us to move forward in some manner of partnership.

I need to begin with a disclaimer. I'm a total amateur at this kind of Jungian analysis. I have no training in it. I haven't (yet) done any men's work based on archetypes (such as the Mankind Project). I recall reading Jung as a teenager and being profoundly impressed; his work on archetypes seemed to carry a deep and incontrovertible truth. Since then I've dabbled, reading Robert Bly's *Iron John* some twenty years ago and more recently, something of Robert Moore and Doug Gillette's work, *King, Warrior, Magician, Lover* (KWML). I'll draw on this particular framework now as it seems ostensibly to offer some fertile insights.

Jung first developed the idea that within all of us, men and women, are masculine and feminine aspects: the animus and anima, respectively. He argued that there are four levels of development to these, a kind of progression to greater maturity or integration of aspects of one's personality. The KWML model is built upon this work and its archetypes broadly correspond to the four levels that Jung devised. However it attributes no order, hierarchy or rank to the different archetypes; they are all equally important. (There are, however, levels of maturity or progression existing within each). This seems to me to be a more useful framework, especially when making comparisons, as I'm about to do (with reservations).

The Moore and Gillette model is essentially of male archetypes. However, because we all hold within us both masculine and feminine aspects, the KWML archetypes reside in every human being. Indeed I believe that Saritha and I both illustrate this point very well – that my anima (feminine) and her animus (masculine) are both very well developed aspects of our respective inner selves. Now I'm going to be so bold as to suggest that Saritha is very much aligned with the Warrior archetype, but with a good sprinkling of the Magician as well. And I believe that I am very much aligned with the Lover archetype, but with a touch of the King thrown in for good measure. What does this tell us about our respective behaviours?

Well, the Warrior is full of energy, which s/he uses in fighting battles, but also is a source of spiritual growth and transformation. Indeed the Warrior is fiercely committed to the transpersonal. The Warrior's domain is the battlefield where s/he fights causes, whatever they may be. But equally, or perhaps more importantly, the battlefield is where s/he strives for spiritual realisation. The Warrior fights campaigns of destruction, but the mature Warrior destroys only that which is harmful in the world. (The immature or 'shadow' Warrior wreaks havoc and destroys that which is good; s/he plays out the bully, the coward or the sado-masochist.) Furthermore, the Warrior is detached, very detached. S/he is way too busy chasing a mission and fighting battles to be concerned with family or relationships.

All of these traits are very clearly identifiable in Saritha: her commitment to her purpose, her spiritual path; her mission to bring positive change to the world; her detachment, especially when she's away 'fighting battles;' and her subsequent sacrificing (or even sabotaging) of her relationships with both her family and with me. Unfortunately for me, my admiration and support for the positive, mature Warrior in Saritha leaves me vulnerable to the proclivities of the shadow. There is no doubt that the immature Warrior in Saritha has the capacity to completely destroy our relationship, despite, or perhaps because of, it being so good.

And what of her Magician? The mature Magician is the wise one, the shaman, the oracle – the knower of secrets. These traits too are very much Saritha and I love her for that. I remember writing of her appearing to me exactly as a magician when she first presented Dragon Dreaming. I've written often of the esoteric knowledge and understanding that she has shared with me and how I have grown in my understanding as a result. I can not imagine, for example, that I could have written such a post as this before Saritha entered my life. For this growth I will forever be grateful; I'm a changed man as a result. But the shadow side of the Magician is the Manipulator and the Trickster. These characteristics have also presented in our interaction. She's entirely capable of using language and behaviour for manipulative effect. I've written of this too.

And what of me? Well, I'm definitely predominantly the Lover. As well as I know myself, I feel I could do no better in describing the inner me than to quote the following:

> *The lover is finely attuned to the realm of the senses and worships beauty. He is a musician, poet and artist, and a lover of all things, both inner and outer. He is passionate, and delights in touching and being touched. He wants to always stay connected, and does not recognise boundaries.* [1]

---

[1] Eivind Figenschau Skjellum, *King, Warrior, Magician, Lover* (KWML) –

This is me to a tee. I am an architect with a finely tuned appreciation of aesthetics, music and visual beauty. In matters of the heart, I am passionate and sensual. And I have a deep fascination with all things erotic. I love to be in connection, hate disconnection and I am very capable of breaching other people's boundaries. The shadow side of this archetype is the addicted Lover. That is me too; I've often said that I have an addictive personality. I love to be in love and I strongly desire sensual gratification. As an aside, I have been progressively refining my diet in recent years, giving up alcohol five years ago, caffeine three years ago and sugar one year ago.[1] Currently, I'm transitioning into becoming vegan. My motivation has always been the seeking of congruence. It's been a spiritual journey of sorts – seeking alignment between body, mind and spirit. Put simply, not wanting to have my body cravings pulling me in one direction and my mind resisting and pushing against the urges. And in the process, I have discovered a spirituality I didn't know I had. So in the framework set by Moore and Gillette, at least in respect of diet, I have been progressing from the immature Lover to the integrated Lover in all his fullness.

But what of the King in me? The King archetype is the source of order and justice. I recognise this in myself immediately; I am borderline OCD in respect of order and passionate about fairness in all things. I am a card carrying egalitarian, socialist and humanist and have been all my life. The King can be selfless, putting the good of his people ahead of his own needs. I also recognise this in myself and I'm sure Saritha does too. Indeed, I believe she hates the self-sacrifice in me. The shadow side of the King is, of course, the Tyrant, the Conqueror and the Possessor. And this side of me we have also seen in earlier posts. It has several times shown

---

archetypes of the mature masculine. See http://www.masculinity-movies.com/articles/king-warrior-magician-lover
[1] For more about my diet, see
http://findhornblog.wordpress.com/2014/08/09/on-diet/

itself in our lovemaking and indeed, could be said to lie behind my jealousy – my desire to 'own' Saritha, as she would see it. The Tyrant in me is an aspect of which I had limited awareness before I met Saritha. She has been a catalyst; indeed, she has encouraged me to explore my shadow, my 'dark side.' I now feel much more integrated as a result of this work. There is another aspect to the King's shadow – that of the Abdicator. This I've been aware of all my life – that I often chose flight over fight when the going gets tough. Saritha has worked with me on this too. Again, I'm extremely grateful to her for her perception and support.

I think that's enough for now. This post has felt like a very useful unpacking; it rings true. It has helped me recognise some of the underlying forces at work in the interpersonal dynamics of our relationship. It feels like material on which we could build greater understanding and perhaps regain trust. It might even be the basis for the rebuilding of a partnership of sorts and/or another project.

BREAKING UP GRACEFULLY

July 27th, 2014

Saritha has been back in the community, staying in my house, for four days that seem like forty; such a lot has happened. Not least, this is due to us having attended the second workshop on *Love, Sex and Intimacy*, which finished today.

She landed on Thursday afternoon at Aberdeen airport; I picked her up. Our reunion was gentle and familiar – loving but not overtly so. She felt somewhat distant. She spent most of the two hour journey home telling me of her adventures of the previous week. She did in the end decide to go to Spain. But on arrival at the airport, discovered that her flight had been cancelled. I received a rare, somewhat desperate, text message from her at the time, saying she was sitting on the floor at the airport, not knowing what to do.

It seems that God really does work in mysterious ways. The cancellation provided Saritha with an opportunity to 'take care of unfinished business' – to go to *Schloss Templehoff*, the home of the friend/lover she'd spent the night with at ZEGG. He and his wife live there as part of a new (four-year-old) intentional community of about one hundred members. I won't elaborate on the nature of her adventures there; that's a story for her to tell. Suffice to say that she enjoyed herself, sexually with the both of them. Hearing this was no surprise. She had told me she was going there and I had little doubt that she would engage sexually. But I found it curious that such an adventure only occurred due to a cancelled flight. It all seemed so circumstantial.

The experience had a deep effect on her, so much so that she was still 'back there,' mentally and emotionally, for the first day or two after returning. So whilst we engaged and reconnected with some tenderness, she wasn't fully present. As a result, we didn't talk too much about the status of our relationship; we 'parked' the discussion for the moment. She did volunteer however, that she felt 'we had a lot to talk about' in a tone which suggested to me that she had already made some decisions about the next steps. I too was feeling resolved, in that I was clear that something was going to have to radically change if our relationship was to continue at all.

We didn't have sex on the first night. Her period had arrived at the same time she had, but in any case, she was clearly disinclined. I found it very challenging lying next to her, the woman I love so deeply and find so damned sexually attractive, with little physical contact or even much cuddling. It firmed my resolve even more – that we needed to talk as soon as possible about whether we were going to be together or not, and if so, in what way?

The next day I took the morning off work; we had the workshop in the afternoon. During the morning we did some processing. Saritha encouraged me to explore the challenge I felt in lying next to her, but not being able to engage sexually. What was the deeper source of my frustration? As part of the process, we acted out what I believe is a Tantra exercise, whereby the man sucks the nipple(s) of his lover as a breastfeeding baby would. In doing so, I had a moment of profound realisation and felt deep healing in a truly embodied way. I accessed early childhood trauma around separation and abandonment that I had no idea I'd been harbouring for some sixty odd years. It made sense of my being so sexually driven all my life. Sex has been the main means by which I've felt reconnected and whole again. What a revelation! Saritha was compassionate and supportive. Once again, I was very grateful for her perception and the intervention.

The workshop began gently; the first day was just a warm up for what was to follow. In the evening and the next morning (after another night without much physical contact) we did some preliminary processing around the status of our relationship. Saritha talked about needing 'space' for herself. I talked about needing reciprocity, kindness and respect. We discussed breaking up, that our respective needs were just too far apart and that it was perhaps the right thing to do in the circumstances. After a little more processing, we came closer together, regained some trust and shared some sensuality. We talked about re-engaging sexually, but thought it best to wait until after the workshop. Perhaps we would create a ritual in a few nights' time.

The next morning's workshop session began powerfully with a group exercise. The women in the room lined up facing the men and openly expressed their inherited rage as victims of millennia of patriarchal domination and violence. The screaming and embodied hostility was extreme. The resultant shame and guilt expressed by some of the men was also very deep. It was intense. Then suddenly, there in the middle, were Saritha and I engaging directly, both as a couple and as representatives of past generations of women and men respectively. She had the opportunity to let fly and she grabbed it with all her power. She gave me hell, both verbally and then physically. I've never seen her so overtly hostile and I hope not to ever again. The essence of what she said was that I was no match for her – not able to meet and stand side by side with her Warrior in battle. This wasn't new, but the ferocity with which it was delivered certainly was. It shocked some of the people in the room, including the facilitator who spent the rest of the weekend checking in with me to see if I was ok (which I was).

Saritha and I have discussed our essential archetypal incompatibility, that which I raised in the last chapter, many times. It is the price I have paid more than once in my life for being attracted to strong, intelligent, articulate, self-possessed women – that on some levels, I am not able to match them. Unfortunately, I was so completely thrown by the ferocity of Saritha's rage that I wasn't able to respond appropriately. My response was some mealy-mouthed notion of being up for the challenge and willing to do the necessary work on myself in order to develop the Warrior in me. What rubbish!! In retrospect, I should have said something like, "I have no intention of meeting your Warrior. This is not me. My archetypal nature is that of the Lover. I'm proud of that and if the immensity of my love is not enough for you, then you can just fuck off!" Better to have had the realisation retrospectively than not at all, and to be able to tell Saritha the next day that this is my truth. She said, "Yes absolutely. If you'd said that at the time, you would have been showing me the Warrior in you."

Anyway, the experience further convinced me that there was no possibility of a partnership, or perhaps even a friendship, with this woman. It was essentially over between us. Such was the apparent depth of her feeling that there seemed to be no way back for us and I think the same was clear to everyone else in the room. After the session, the facilitator took us aside and counselled us, suggesting that we should not process any further that evening, but rather wait until the next morning. She thought we needed to 'let things settle' overnight. The afternoon session was devoted to small group work. Saritha and I didn't engage much at all, nor had we over lunch. I was feeling the gulf between us and I was in pain. So much so, that I resolved to call an end to the relationship as soon as possible – as soon as we got home. And perhaps even ask her to find somewhere else to stay, even from that night onward. The thought of another night like the previous two was just too much to bear.

So that's what we did. At my prompting, we talked and quickly agreed to split up. I asked her to find an alternative place to stay and she said that would be no problem, but in any case, she intended spending the night in nature with her sleeping bag, doing a vision quest. We decided to do a ritual there and then, whereby we would each make a *macquette*[1] that symbolically represented all that we wished to let go from the relationship (the negative aspects) and then we would burn them. And we would also write and/or speak appreciations for what had been valuable and was worth honouring about our relationship. I was in a fog of sadness, bordering on despair. Was this really going to be the end? Was I never going to make love with this sexual goddess again?

We made the *macquettes*; me reluctantly. I saw the value in the ritual well enough, but had no energy or enthusiasm for anything, let alone a creative act of model making – something which normally I'd greatly enjoy. We burned our *macquettes* in the firebox of the wood stove in my living room. And then we exchanged and read our cards inscribed with beautiful and touching appreciations. It was a powerful moment; there was magic in it. We embraced with immense depth of feeling. And then what should happen? We fell into a long, deep and sensual kiss – a kiss that carried all of the love and joy and gratitude that we had for each other and for the experience of the previous three months together. And it spoke of our mutually strong sexual attraction. We went to bed and made love, slowly and beautifully. Then Saritha went out with her sleeping bag, but she returned to the warmth of our bed at about one or two in the morning due to rain and cold. The next morning we made love again, this time more powerfully. I was in my full masculine power. Saritha commented that this is when she does glimpse the Warrior in me, when we're in bed together.

So now it seemed, we were split up, but still sexually active. This wasn't what I was expecting at all! But what joy I felt and what peace of mind. In a way it felt like the best possible outcome. We talked laughingly about becoming occasional, *ad hoc* lovers. Not a couple, not partners or even

---

[1] A scale model made, in this case, from cardboard.

friends, necessarily; just lovers. I've been feeling totally at peace ever since (although it's been less than a day); feeling completely unattached to outcomes. We have been happy and loving together, engaging with ease and warmth. I think that in this realignment of our relationship we'll find much greater mutuality. Our sexual attraction has always been a primary motivation for our being together, so why not just acknowledge that fully? We'll be polyamourous and it will be by mutual choice. It feels like we have finally reached a place of peace and understanding and I think that whatever unfolds from here is likely to serve us both, and the highest good. It feels like we have been, after all, successfully engaged in peace work, doing our bit to heal the rift between all men and women. This is the world work that we talked of back when we designed our one month long project together. This has been our underlying motivation for doing and going through what we did and for the documenting and disseminating. It feels great to have now cleared away all of the extraneous and useless needs, wants, attachments and expectations.

I am, we both are, very grateful for all that's been, all that is and all that will be.

BREAKING UP LESS THAN GRACEFULLY

July 29th, 2014

It's over. Saritha has moved out. We have fallen from grace yet again. Last night we clashed over something that could easily have been avoided with greater sensitivity (from me) and clearer communication (from her). Ironically, what began as a project in conscious relationship, founded due to a lack of consciousness. I don't want to post mortem here. Suffice to say (again) that I believe what we missed in these last weeks was the quality of the container we had created in June. We threw together a token container in ZEGG and had none at all in these last days. So we paid the price. It seems, at least for us, that consciousness needs to be deliberately held within a strong container and is unlikely to prevail otherwise. Without consciousness, we fell back into old behaviour patterns – destructive, irreconcilable patterns that overwhelmed the more subtle qualities of our relationship such as forgiveness, grace and generosity of spirit. And sadly, it seems that the love itself wasn't enough. That's my take on it anyway.

I'm feeling sad and disappointed right now, but also quite centred and strong. I hope and believe we can continue with some manner of relationship, but it's probably going to take a while for that to emerge if, indeed, it ever does. I know full well what happens when Saritha is elsewhere – she drops off the radar. I believe now that this really will be the last (or last but one) post. However, I'll be delighted beyond words if it is not.

NOT A POST MORTEM:
JUST A FEW REFLECTIONS

July 30th, 2014

In the last few days I've been seeking answers to the questions: What went wrong? What changed? What happened? How could we have had such a beautiful, pure and good thing going during the month of June, only to fall to such depths of anger, frustration and recrimination during July? When I asked this of Saritha, she simply said, "The honeymoon ended!" There's truth in this. Irrespective of the container we created, we were 'in heaven' back then, in good part because we didn't know each other that well. I had hoisted Saritha onto the highest of pedestals, a place from where she could not fail to fall and she had not perceived those aspects of my personality that ultimately caused her disillusion. Once the 'honeymoon' was over and without the support of a safe container, we were each unable to accept the shadow in the other. In that sense, our aspiration to grow into unconditional love remained unfulfilled. And perhaps it was precisely because we once flew so high that the unravelling was so sudden and so dramatic. It's a long way down from heaven.

The learning and the lessons for me are numerous and I've covered many of them in earlier posts, but to recap, I learned of the depth of my emotional life on both sides of the ledger;

the light and the dark. And I learned that all of it, every experience within and without, carries opportunity for further growth and understanding. Most recently, I learned about early childhood experiences (of which I had no prior knowledge) that may well have established compulsive life-long behaviour patterns. I learned, for example, of my tendency to become attached, if not addicted, to both the object of my love/desire and to outcomes. I believe this phenomenon has been called limerence. And of course, it has been like a red rag to the bull in Saritha who so values, almost above all else, her independence and freedom. Equally damaging has been my propensity for taking responsibility for the other, which Saritha saw and felt as controlling. These behaviours may well have been established in the first few years of my life.

My mother told me yesterday of the sudden (cold turkey) weaning I'd endured as a ten-week-old baby, ordered by her doctor, because of a breast infection. Apparently, I was in a state of complete trauma, almost certainly feeling abandonment, perhaps even annihilation, for some weeks. This may well account for my sometimes desperate need to be and stay in connection with the object of my love, which in combination with Saritha's equally strong drive to disconnect, was my greatest challenge of the last month. As mentioned above, it may also account for my being so sexually driven all of my life – that for me, sex is the means by which I feel reconnected and made whole. Mum also told me of a period when I was about three. She was a twenty-two year old with three kids, of whom I was the eldest. My brother was desperately sick with asthma and my sister was a baby. Then dad went overseas for three months on business. She confirmed that my desire to protect and take responsibility for others (i.e. be controlling, as Saritha would see it) was firmly established at this time. Indeed, my earliest childhood memory is of my brother's illness and wanting to make it better. It seems I adopted the surrogate male protector role, even as a three-year-old.

I wrote at some length about our archetypal differences,

Saritha and I, in the post, *On Archetypes*; that her persona is primarily of the Warrior, whilst mine is predominantly of the Lover. Our respective needs and wants in these roles seem ostensibly to be so far apart as to be totally incompatible. Be that as it may, I realise that I have work to do on myself in order to address some of my compulsions and to heal. There will be opportunities for that in the coming months. I intend to book a session or two with the woman who facilitated the workshops we attended. Her process and constellation work should help me to further unpack these early childhood experiences and I also intend to sign up for an introductory weekend of the Mankind Project (MKP), which happens to be coming to our neighbourhood in November. MKP works closely with archetypes; its three-day intensive helps men to develop their Warrior and become more integrated. I think I can benefit from that. I'm smiling as I write this. I've avoided deep work on myself until quite late in life. My ex-wife, bless her, was always on about the need, but I was otherwise convinced. I've always felt happy in my skin. I'll write to her soon in acknowledgement. However, it's better late than never. I have a taste for personal growth now that I didn't have three months ago and I have Saritha and our journey together to thank for that.

Having said all that, I believe that in one important respect I contributed brilliantly to our three month long love affair. That is, with my capacity for open-hearted loving. It's amazing how the universe provides. When I sat down to write this post, I felt completely uninspired, not knowing where to start. Distracted, I turned to Facebook and immediately saw the quote below pop up in my news feed. It felt like a sign, a divine message of reassurance that actually, my crazy, reckless, fearless and open-hearted way of loving, of falling and being 'in love,' is perfectly ok. And that to show up, do my best and just be ME is enough. In fact, it's plenty! I'd been thinking that I stuffed up with Saritha; that I loved her too much, too enthusiastically and too deeply for my own good and for hers. But the quote says otherwise and it resonates.

Dear Human: You've got it all wrong. You didn't come here to master unconditional love. That is where you came from and where you'll return. You came here to learn personal love. Universal love. Messy love. Sweaty love. Crazy love. Broken love. Whole love. Infused with divinity. Lived through the grace of stumbling. Demonstrated through the beauty of... messing up. Often. You didn't come here to be perfect. You already are. You came here to be gorgeously human. Flawed and fabulous. And then to rise again into remembering. But unconditional love? Stop telling that story. Love, in truth, doesn't need ANY other adjectives. It doesn't require modifiers. It doesn't require the condition of perfection. It only asks that you show up. And do your best. That you stay present and feel fully. That you shine and fly and laugh and cry and hurt and heal and fall and get back up and play and work and live and die as YOU. It's enough. It's Plenty. Courtney A. Walsh

RECONNECTION 3

Early August, 2014

Saritha was booked into Experience Week, starting on the Saturday following her move out on Tuesday, July 29th.[1] So she needed somewhere to live for the remainder of the week. I learned later that she went to stay with a friend in Findhorn Village. There she spent several days in quiet reflection and recovery. She rested, slept, wrote, drew, chatted, exchanged massages with her friend and talked about relationships. Those few days, she later said, were very healing. As for me, I thought about Saritha constantly and missed her deeply, but I was convinced that our separation was final and for the best. I was sure that the relationship was forever over.

On the following Sunday, I was working outside in the garden when one of the many tour groups that pass my house every week happened by. As often occurs, the tour guide stopped to view and discuss my house from the road. It

---

[1] The previous chapter was the final post on the blog. For the next three months I wrote nothing more. I'd become somewhat disillusioned and was not inspired to write. However, in early November Saritha and I revived our intention to document and disseminate; we decided to publish this book. Together, we reviewed and recalled what had happened since the end of July, which I then wrote up retrospectively. This accounts for the change from present back to past tense for the remainder of the book.

suddenly dawned on me that this could be Saritha's Experience Week group, as they often tour the Park[1] on a Sunday afternoon. So I moved from the porch where I was watering plants towards the street to get a better view of the group. And there, sure enough, I saw Saritha standing at the back of the group looking like she didn't want to be there – withdrawn and reticent with downcast eyes. My heart jumped, I was so happy to see her, although I imagined and could anyway see, that my feelings were not being reciprocated.

Saritha had both wanted and not wanted to be there, she told me later. She'd not wanted to go on the tour as she already knew the Park well. In that sense it would be a waste of time, but she went out of her sense of responsibility to the group and also, in part, because she half hoped she might run into me and that we might find time for a check-in. As the tour neared my house, she felt both dread and desire at the thought of seeing me. She held back, hoping to remain invisible at the rear of the group. And yet, when the tour stopped at my house, there I was, talking with the tour leader and scanning the group for a view of her.

I picked a flower from a hanging basket, a beautiful double fuchsia, a species that I knew Saritha found fascinating. And as the group moved off, I walked slowly toward her and held out my humble offering. She looked up directly into my face, didn't smile, but didn't turn away either; just held my gaze with a soft and sad look. My heart melted; I wanted to embrace her, but thought better of it. Best, I thought, to invite her in for a cup of tea. It's not often she refuses such an invitation. And so it was, to my great delight, that she accepted; she abandoned the tour and followed me hesitantly into the house.

Our check-in led to a softening of thoughts and feelings, as they so often had done in the past. After a while, Saritha repositioned herself on the couch so as to be able to lie in my

---

[1] The Park is the name given to our main campus in Findhorn. It was a caravan park when we purchased it (and still is), hence the name.

arms. After a while more, as the energy passing between us built, she looked up and gently kissed me. It was the moment my body had craved ever since she left so abruptly a week earlier; and it triggered all of the desire and longing that I'd been harbouring since. My hormones kicked in and I kissed her back with somewhat more passion than she'd expressed toward me. (So what else is new?) "NO!" she protested. She jumped up, hurriedly gathered up her bag and coat and ran dramatically out of the door. I didn't even have time to respond before she'd disappeared up the road. I was somewhat stunned, and angry at myself for having blown the opportunity for reconciliation. But also, I was bemused by the drama of the scene, seeing it as something from a melodramatic, rom-com film script.

That night I went to 5Rhythms[1] in the hall, hoping that the dancing would shift the pain, guilt and frustration I was feeling. I began the dance with a slow circumnavigation of the floor in a semi-comatose state of confusion and then another and another. The fog in my head wasn't shifting. I couldn't rid my mind of the sight of Saritha sprinting out of the door like a frightened rabbit. I was feeling guilty and stupid and unable to shift the confusion. Then it came to me. If 5Rhythms wasn't going to help, then the only thing that might would be a late night visit to Cluny[2] to see her. So I left mid-session without saying anything to the dance teacher. I didn't want to have to explain myself – what I was feeling seemed so inexplicable.

I went home and booked a car from the carpool, showered and changed, then headed for Cluny. I knew that Saritha's Experience Week group was holding an attunement that evening and that their session would finish around 9pm.

---

[1] 5Rhythms is a contemporary dance form popular around the world. See http://www.5rhythms.com for more information.
[2] Cluny Hill is the name of our second campus in Forres, five miles from Findhorn. It's a large Victorian hotel with accommodation for over 100. Cluny is the venue for many of our programmes including the majority of Experience Weeks.

I got there just beforehand. I knew they were in the Beechtree Room so I went to the adjacent library from where I could see comings and goings. I waited... and waited. I was conflicted. I wasn't sure how welcome would be my out-of-the-blue appearance. I thought that if she took it badly, my boldness might completely blow my chances; she might think I was stalking her. And how was I to meet her as she emerged from the Beechtree Room without making a scene in front of the rest of the group? I mulled over all of this, thinking increasingly I was really crazy to be there, feeling like leaving immediately and going back to the Park. But no, I thought, I'm going to see this through.

At around 9.30, the first person emerged from the Beechtree Room. And who should it be but her! What a break, I thought, I can confront her before the rest of the group follows. But before I had time to act, she disappeared down a few steps and into a long corridor. I followed, but in the fifteen seconds it took me to get there she had completely disappeared. I heard someone in a bathroom a few doors along the corridor. I couldn't be sure, but I guessed it must be her. How else could she disappear so quickly? So I waited... and waited... and waited what seemed like an eternity until, eventually, Saritha emerged. Suddenly, there we were, face-to-face. She was, of course, shocked to see me, but the look of surprise disappeared more quickly that I expected and it wasn't replaced with a look of anger or outrage. Rather, she looked at me blankly and asked simply, "What are you doing here?" "I've come to see you," I said, "Can we talk?" I thought I saw the flicker of a half smile across her face, but wasn't sure. But in any case I was relieved that she hadn't burst into a tirade of abuse. Instead, she asked me to wait whilst she went back to the Beechtree Room. Apparently, the session wasn't yet over.

Eventually, the group emerged and she came for me. She wasn't going to take me to her room, so we looked around for somewhere to meet for a check-in. We found an empty reading room where we sat in semi-darkness and talked. It seemed she wasn't mad at me at all for being so presumptuous. In fact, she was touched. She alluded to fair maidens being rescued from castles by brave knights. Indeed, Cluny is a castle of sorts. We talked and talked, for a long time and predictably, we grew close. We cuddled in chairs that weren't conducive. We kissed. I was filled with gratitude for the willingness that we were both showing and the grace of the situation. It seemed that love would indeed prevail. We agreed to meet on the coming Wednesday evening; the only free night she had in the week.

I drove home from Cluny in a state of ecstasy.

RETURN TO RELATIONSHIP

Mid August, 2014

Saritha came over for dinner on the following Wednesday night. She caught the 5.30pm bus and was at my place by 6. I'd bought the ingredients for a meal of roast vegetables and steamed greens. We cooked together; something we'd done often in June, but little since. For me, our collaborative cooking was both a joy and a challenge; we're both quite attached to our own workflows, which oftentimes didn't sync. However, the cooking and the evening flowed graciously. It felt like we were back in some kind of bubble, happy to be reconnected once more. And of course, I was ecstatic at the thought of spending the night with Saritha in the inner sanctum of my house – our adopted temple of love.

In the morning, I dropped her back at Cluny. Some of her Experience Week friends were hanging about the entrance. I perceived some quizzical looks, which I surmised were probably due to them thinking (on the basis of Saritha's sharings with the group) that we had broken up. On the contrary, it felt to me that we'd fully returned to relationship again and I was in heaven.

Saritha enjoyed Experience Week more than either of us was expecting. I feared she might find it boring as she'd participated in so many workshops of a similar nature in the past; indeed she had facilitated similar such processes and programmes herself. But to the contrary, she really enjoyed the week, in particular the sharings by several members of the community on aspects of their lives in Findhorn. She enjoyed the programme as a whole – the integration of various activities into a coherent package that carried participants on a heart-opening and transformative journey. She talked of the joy of working in Cluny gardens and of an occasion where she was pruning back dead growth. She wept as she thought of the work as a metaphor for the inner work of transformation – clearing out the old in order to birth the new. I felt grateful for her landing in the Foundation with grace and enthusiasm. It was improving the chances of her staying around.

For Saritha, Experience Week was followed by another week-long course, Exploring Community Life (ECL). ECL is designed to deepen a participant's understanding of the Foundation and our community culture – it involves a lot of education. Saritha was the sole participant that week so had the exclusive attention of her focaliser, an articulate and intelligent man with a public service background and a good understanding of the governance and 'political' machinations of the Foundation. He was a good match for Saritha, I thought; they would have many a long and deep conversation about important things. And so it transpired. She learned much from him that further deepened her connection with the Foundation.

Midway through the week I paid her a visit. We met in her room and decided to take a bath together. Cluny, a once thriving Victorian spa, is famous for the size of its baths; they are perfect in their dimensions for two. That night, in the bath and then on the floor of the bathroom we enjoyed some of the hottest, raunchiest lovemaking of our short sex lives. What was tricky was keeping the noise level down. We were conscious of the possibility of others passing by in the corridor but in any case, there is a 10pm curfew on bath-taking, which we had well transgressed.

With our sexual connection well and truly remade, I felt more confident that our relationship was back on track. As for Saritha, her sights were set on higher, more spiritual, things (as they have been all along). After I left her that night, she went to the Sanctuary to meditate. There, alone in the quietness of that sacred space, she experienced something quite profound – an encounter with the unseen, 'angelic' realms.

On the previous day she'd attuned to (i.e. been successfully interviewed for) the FF programme that logically follows on from ECL. Called Living in Community as a Guest (LCG), it offers guests a course that is rich in group time and education as well as participation, more-or-less full-time, in a work department – what we refer to as 'work is love in action.' During a meditation, which in Findhorn is an intrinsic part of an attunement, her interviewer had a vision of Saritha lying as a naked baby, defenceless and vulnerable, only to be approached by a great presence that somehow wrapped itself around her in protection.

And so it was, late the following night, as she sat in meditation, that Saritha had a strong visceral experience. She felt herself falling backwards (she was seated cross-legged on the floor) only to be 'caught' in the embrace of a large, powerful, unseen being that she identified as the Angel of Cluny, or perhaps the Angel of Findhorn. For an interminable period, perhaps minutes, it wrapped itself around her and held her in a gesture of love and support. In those powerful moments, Saritha felt as if she'd fully arrived into the culture of Findhorn and was being welcomed and encouraged by both seen and unseen beings to deepen her relationship with the Foundation. From that moment, she was no longer here in Findhorn, even in part, because of her relationship with me. Rather she was in a new partnership with the Foundation. It was as if I had 'given her away,' as a father might a daughter at a marriage, to the new love in her life.

Paradoxically perhaps, I was delighted to hear this and

even to feel the consequent shift in our relationship. Because I am so enamoured of my life here in Findhorn and my role in the Findhorn Foundation, I naturally wished the same for the woman I love so much, even if it meant that her focus was shifting away from our relationship. And I reasoned also, in my more self-serving moments, that this deepening of her connection with the community would ensure that she would remain as a presence in my life into the indefinite future.

WAVES

In late August, something happened that induced another shift in the dynamics of our relationship. My previous partner, with whom I'd had a seven year long relationship and still had a strong friendship, returned to the Park to live. She'd been away as a full-time student for most of the previous five years. I left Saritha in bed early on the 23rd to drive to St Andrews. I was to spend the weekend helping my friend pack and then bring her back to Findhorn. Saritha told me afterwards that she felt abandoned at the time; as if I'd gone off to rescue a different princess.

My friend and I arrived back in the Park late in the afternoon on August 24th. We were preparing some food when Saritha turned up at the door. She'd ostensibly come to take her computer away, having left it on the coffee table earlier in the day. We'd seen it when we arrived and surmised that Saritha would likely show up to collect it at some point. On some level, I think she left it there deliberately so as to have an excuse to come around to meet, or perhaps confront, my friend.

Things were awkward when she walked in. I was conflicted. How could I greet Saritha with my usual level of affection and not hurt my friend. I knew she was already suffering at what she imagined was the loss, or potential loss, of my friendship on account of the new woman in my life. Saritha was hurt by my failing to kiss, hug or even touch her on arrival. She left with the computer, but came back almost immediately. She had trouble even walking away knowing that there was unsaid stuff swirling between the three of us; confusion that needed to be cleared.

We held a three way check-in. It went well. We were each able to express what had previously been unsaid and Saritha left feeling somewhat resolved. My friend was, I think, even more confused than before. She just didn't understand Saritha's attitude to relationships and her research into combining love and freedom, even though she and I had happily been in an open relationship for several years. The three of us met again for another check-in some days later. This time it was in a very public place, outside the CC. We drove at least one mutual friend from the table, because of the intensity of the situation. And again, Saritha tried to explain her worldview; she was seeking acceptance and understanding, but to no avail. If anything, it seemed to further confuse my ex-partner and estrange the two of them even more.

My ex didn't want to move back in with me even if just to sleep on the couch. My relationship with Saritha had impacted on her connection with my house (in which she had once resided) as well as with me. So I used my three-week allocation of guest accommodation in Foundation housing to ensure that she had a roof over her head for at least that long. Following that, she moved in with friends and then to the Village where she more or less disappeared from view, much to the frustration of Saritha who remained keen to engage with her and for the three of us to work something out. But it was never clear to any of us what that might be.

DREAMING 2

Early Sept, 2014
Saritha and I talked a lot about the varying dynamics and qualities of our relationship in the periods before, during and after our comings and goings from Germany. This has been one of our great strengths i.e. our willingness to stand outside our relationship and make an assessment of what might better serve it (as opposed to us individually or together). We concluded that we'd struggled in July and August for want of a well-defined container; the kind we'd created back in June. So we resolved to restore some of the consciousness to our project via another round of Dragon Dreaming. DD is, after all, conceived as an iterative process.

We sat down at my place one night to begin the process over again: The Dreaming, Planning, Doing and Celebration. And we began as before with an intention.

INTENTION 2
The intention of this project is to stay in connection in a way that serves each of us, whilst we endeavour to move towards peace between the genders.

This is quite a different intention from our first, which was: *To create a one month long safe container for our relationship that serves each of us individually and together as well as our community and the Earth.* The first intention underpinned the initial month-long phase of our project, which was to dive deep into love, sex and intimacy within a limited period. The reference in the second intention to 'peace between the genders' is what underpins our aspiration to combine partnership (with one person) with freedom (to explore sexually with others). This has been the focus of our relationship since early July when we went to ZEGG. This second intention, therefore, signifies the beginning of a new phase of our project in conscious relationship, which entails, if I may quote Saritha here, 'action research into new ways of being in a relationship that are in line with the planetary transition we are going through.'

We immediately followed up the intention setting with a Dreaming Circle.

DREAMING 2

G: That we come together to share and grow our love.

S: That it brings a lot of joy and fulfilment.

G: That it enables us to be accepted by each other as our true selves.

S: That we have freedom and intimacy at the same time.

G: That we are able to freely express our needs and wants.

S: That we take ownership of our emotions, reactions and desires.

S: That we take full responsibility for our personal development and behaviour.

G: That we come together only when it suits us both.

S: That we perceive and respect each other's boundaries.

G: That we strive to keep the channels of communication open and endeavour to address disharmony promptly.

S: That we practice our 1st, 2nd and 3rd awareness.

G: That we treat each other with care and respect.

S: That we are free to explore sexually with others, as long as we keep in communication.

G: That we don't have any expectations beyond being in the here and now.

S: That we don't put pressure on each other or claim ownership of one another.

G: That we strive to come from a place of love rather than a place of fear.

S: That we seek external help whenever necessary to deal with challenges.

G: That we continue to explore sexually and to push our sexual boundaries.

S: That we continue to explore tools, methods and techniques to investigate sex, love, intimacy and relationships.

G: That this project runs for the duration that Saritha stays in Findhorn.

S: That we re-evaluate this on a regular basis.

G: That we release each other entirely when we are geographically separated. That we have no expectation or obligation to communicate with each other when we are away.

S: That we aspire to hold, accept and acknowledge each other's shadows, understanding that there's no need to rescue, fix or make it better for the other.

S: That we continue to develop our spiritual connection through rituals and practices.

S: That we play the Transformation Game together.

So having spent the two months since being at ZEGG without much definition to our project, let alone a safe container for our relationship, we had now launched a new phase of our exploration with a focus on 'liberated love' or ZEGG styled polyamoury. We'd struggled over the previous two months for want of a Dragon Dreaming inspired formulation. Now, at least, we had one again. And, whilst this new phase was mutually agreed, it was championed mostly by Saritha. I think that comes through if one reads between the lines of the above Dreaming Circle. I have, in fact, considerably more experience of free love than her, having practiced it in a low-key way ever since I first went to ZEGG thirteen years ago. I have an intellectual interest in, and commitment to, polyamoury – or at least I have had in recent years. However I already sensed, based on what unfolded at ZEGG back in July, that this particular experiment in combining partnership with freedom was going to challenge me like no other. My head was in favour, but I wondered whether my heart would cope.

Apropos the last line of the Dreaming Circle (that we play the Transformation Game together) Saritha had come to my place a day or two beforehand with a sizeable parcel under her arm. "A present," she said as she passed it to me with a shy smile. It was unlike her to formally give me a gift; it's just not something she generally does. So I was delighted to receive any kind of present from her. To me such a gesture represents more than just an act of generosity, but is somehow symbolic of the value of the relationship to the giver. The gift was a boxed set of the Transformation Game. 'The Game' as it's known in Findhorn is a board game that was created in the 1970s by two members of the community. It's designed as a vehicle for transformation – a means by which individuals and groups can deepen their inner work and self-knowledge. I'd not played The Game much recently, but had enjoyed it on a few occasions in my first few years at Findhorn. Saritha had played during ECL and was very taken with it. She bought it with a view to us playing it together as a means of deepening our connection and infusing our relationship with greater consciousness. I was delighted.

In the week that followed, we played The Game twice: a two hour and a six hour game. (Players generally nominate the length of the game at the outset). On both occasions we both completed the game within fifteen minutes of the nominated time. This, apparently, is a rare occurrence at any time. For us to do so twice, given that we were playing for the benefit of our relationship, was very confirming.

RETURN TO CONFLICT

Early Sept, 2014

Saritha's six weeks in Cluny (including the first month of her LCG) were, in general, very beneficial for our relationship. We would see each other two or three times a week, she was always pleased to see me, we had things to share and most importantly from her perspective, she would have 'space' for her work, her projects and her other relationships. This made her happy and a pleasure to be with. However, toward the end of her term there, storm clouds of old appeared on the horizon.

We were having brunch in the CC one Sunday morning when Saritha noticed across the room a man she had met during the three week period she spent at Newbold House before coming to Findhorn. Newbold is a beautiful Victorian manor house; home to a small residential community of eight or ten people with a strong connection to Findhorn. It is, in fact, a daughter community. Saritha had hung out with him there. They had enjoyed each other's company, purely as friends. She crossed the room to greet him and they conversed for a while. When she came back, she said, "Now that's a man you ought to be jealous of." She wasn't kidding. I learned subsequently that she'd arranged to meet him for a catch up on the following night in Cluny. She didn't tell me at the time; something which she later told me she regretted. In our many months together, it was one of the few transgressions of our agreement to be fully transparent.

As it turned out, I was to be in Cluny the following afternoon for a work-related meeting. So I stayed for dinner and Saritha and I met for a check-in afterwards. It was then that she told me she was meeting this guy that evening – very soon in fact. But she assured me that they were just friends and were simply going to catch up. We finished our check-in around 8pm and I went with her to the lounge to meet him. He and I exchanged pleasantries and I left to go back to the Park. I knew intuitively (indeed feared) that there was more than just a simple catch up on the agenda for the evening.

The next day my suspicions were confirmed when Saritha and I met at morning tea and she told me that she would like a check-in after lunch. That could mean only one thing, I thought. She had something important to tell me and it was about what had transpired the night before. I spent the rest of the morning with a knot in my stomach and a racing mind. To a lesser extent, I was reliving the drama and trauma of our time at ZEGG and Saritha's exploration there with another man. When we met for our check-in she spent an inordinate length of time telling me the story. They had gone for a walk in the garden, it had become dark, they had come indoors to find somewhere to talk, they couldn't find a suitable space (how convenient, I thought) and so she had no choice but to invite him to her room for a chat. There they talked about past relationships, sexuality, etc., etc., etc. I could have written the script myself, and indeed, had done so in my mind already. Eventually, she got around to telling me that they had kissed… but that was all. He had gone home shortly afterward. Well, that's something, I thought, at least they hadn't fucked! She added that they had no plans to meet again and that she wasn't much interested.

So how was I to interpret all this? I felt, and I told her so, that she'd deliberately avoided telling me the truth, both of the arrangement to meet with him and of her intentions. I accused her of deliberately seducing him. She didn't deny it. I was somewhat incredulous of the whole event; it seemed so circumstantial. Had he not been in the CC that Sunday, it would never have happened. So I chose to see the event as a case of Saritha just wanting to express her independence and experience her freedom. I don't believe she really saw the guy as a potential lover, or was even much attracted to him. I think she was just trying it on – acting out the freedom to explore that our project now inherently permitted. And so it transpired that they never met again. I don't think there's even been much communication between them since.

RETURN TO THE PARK

Mid September, 2014

On September 13th, Saritha returned to the Park to live. She had 'served her time' in Cluny, although it must be said that towards the end of her six weeks there, she was feeling quite enamoured of the lifestyle.[1] Being in Cluny supported her spiritual practice; she could access the Sanctuary late at night without having to venture outdoors. Everything is under one roof at Cluny. And aside from the incident with the guy from Newbold, our relationship was stable and nourishing for us both whilst she was there.

Saritha's return to the Park induced a shift in the dynamics between us. She moved into a bungalow named Sunrise,[2] near

---

[1] The first month of LCG is always held in Cluny. Following that, participants can opt to either be in Cluny or the Park.

[2] Perhaps a word of explanation is needed here. It is common for couples in the Findhorn Foundation to have separate rooms, usually in different buildings, as most residential coworkers share a house with up to eight others (and in Cluny, with about forty others) couples generally need a space each, else there is nowhere to go when they want personal privacy or to be alone. This gives them the opportunity to sleep together or not, as they choose. And in our case, Saritha and I had clearly benefited from living separately whilst she was in Cluny, so it made sense to retain that arrangement when she returned to the Park.

the Community Centre. This located her physically in the centre of the community, a place from which she could easily access most of its cultural and recreational offerings. And whether or not this was a factor, Saritha's range of interests and activities began to expand. My house, on the other hand, is in Pineridge, quite close to the centre physically, but remote energetically – a location that I much appreciate for its quietness and proximity to nature. Along with most of the other Foundation coworkers in the Park, I live somewhat remotely from the hurly-burly of daily community life. The ambiguity of the distance between our two dwellings had an unexpected effect on me. I felt that she was just far enough away to be living separately and yet, tantalisingly close enough to be available should I desire to see her – which of course I did most of the time.

Her flatmate in Sunrise was a quiet, sweet woman who had been there for some time prior to Saritha arriving. She was lonely, having not made close friends in the Park. So for her, Saritha's arrival was a godsend. The two of them immediately bonded; they hung out, shared their lives and did craft together. At times this challenged me. On more than a few evenings after coming to my place for dinner or for us to spend time together, Saritha would be drawn back to Sunrise to sleep rather than stay with me overnight out of concern for her flatmate's well-being. I began to resent this. Furthermore, her flatmate became as adoring of Saritha as I had been, and as clingy. It seemed to my immature, needy self that she and I were competing for Saritha's attention. However, I believe this was just a symptom of something bigger.

This period marked the growth of an unhealthy tendency in me. My love for Saritha, it seemed to me, was continuing to deepen and become more intense, as it had been from the outset. And as a consequence, I was feeling drawn, if not compelled, to spend more and more time with her. And also, I sought an experience of her that was increasingly intense. These are clearly symptoms of addiction. With the benefit of hindsight, I recognise in my needs and desires of this period, a growing addiction to the love, sex and intimacy I was enjoying with Saritha but also, to the woman herself.

My addiction, or limerence as I believe it's called, would manifest in different ways. I felt drawn, physically dragged as if by a magnet, into Sunrise to see her whenever I walked past (which was several times a day). I'd seek an embrace, caress or some other acknowledgement whenever I saw her in the CC or elsewhere in the community. All of this was, of course, incendiary as far as she was concerned. Her sense of separateness and independence from me was increasing anyway as she deepened her connection with the Foundation, made new friends and diversified her activities. But in any case, to have me being so 'needy' as she saw it, only served to irritate and alienate her.

In addition to our relationship deteriorating under this strain, we found less and less time for quality interaction. As her life became busier, so did mine; I was working feverishly on an upcoming conference. The quality time we once dedicated to outings, sharing meals and bringing ritual to our relationship seemed to disappear from our growing list of priorities. We were losing the consciousness with which we had so determinedly infused our relationship in its first few months. Was ours going the way of so many others – drifting aimlessly after the honeymoon was over, to eventually degenerate, disintegrate and terminate?

A NEW OLD STORY

Early October, 2014

For a week from September 27th, Findhorn played host to the biggest and most complex conference we've held in twenty years, the *New Story Summit*. About four hundred people attended the week-long event. As a member of the Conference Team of the Findhorn Foundation, I had been centrally involved in its organisation. I'd been under a lot of pressure in the preceding weeks and knew I would be under even more duress during the event itself. After her last engagement with another man, I spoke to Saritha about my concern that she would use the event to further spread her wings – to take the opportunity to connect with one or more of the many eligible male visitors on the guest list. I implored her to have some consideration for my well-being, knowing that such an occurrence would tip me into stress overload. She said she would keep it in mind – that she would treat me with kindness and respect.

My fears were realised on the first day of the conference. I'd been communicating with a particular participant for weeks leading up to the event. He'd had problems with his visa application and needed a UK resident to transfer money for him. This I did twice, from my private bank account (it was the easiest way) at quite some inconvenience. Anyway, when he came to register we greeted. I liked him immediately; he had a certain charisma. I introduced him to Saritha (who needed to talk to him anyway about a craft bazaar she was organising) and went about my business. When I noticed a half hour later that they were still talking in a very engaged way, a thousand alarm bells went off inside my head and my chest contracted around my heart. Uh-oh I thought, here we go again. When I went to them on some pretence, but really to see what the hell was going on, she'd just given him her favourite necklace. "Are you jealous?" Saritha asked, with her most beguiling smile. Absolutely, I thought. I'm not exactly sure what I said; I wasn't thinking straight.

I instigated a check-in at the earliest opportunity. She assured me that the gift of the necklace meant nothing and that I was being overly dramatic with my concerns. I knew I wasn't. She told me later however, that my very concern had planted seeds in her mind – that perhaps this guy was indeed of interest. And sure enough, the next evening around 9pm I get a text message from her to say that they had been for a walk and that nothing had happened, because he was married. She ended the text with a frowning face as if to say, if he hadn't been married she would have happily taken him to bed. At least that's how I interpreted it. In fact, it seemed to me irrelevant that he was married. She'd clearly taken him for a walk with a view to checking out his availability. She was on the prowl once again.

I lay awake all that night in pain and anger. The next morning I blew a gasket. I dismantled the altar that we built together in our 'temple' and threw all of her clothes, the ones she left at my place, into four bags that I dumped at her bungalow. I knew the gesture would make my feelings very clear and I hoped that it would hurt her; I was feeling angry and vengeful. At her instigation, we met later in the day for a check-in. Saritha had indeed been hurt by my simulated 'eviction.' She explained that she had no intention of engaging sexually with this man, but she did want to hang out with him through the week. The reluctance to engage intimately, she explained, was his instigation, as he didn't want to jeopardise his marriage. Saritha, for her part, didn't want to go there either if his wife wasn't informed, such is her commitment to transparency. I was relieved but not deluded. This outcome was, yet again, purely circumstantial – it was due to his being married. It could equally have been different.

I felt that I was going to be too busy through the week to be able to engage with her or them or the situation. I angrily decided to leave them to it and deal with the consequences when the event was over. However, soon enough, we held a prolonged check-in, quite publicly in front of the Universal Hall, the main conference venue. I told her that I felt our relationship had been damaged beyond repair, that it was over and that she had treated me and it (the relationship) with complete disrespect. She got very upset. We engaged with two or three friends who attempted, as best they could, to support us. But I for one wasn't much in the mood for being supported, let alone mediated. Saritha, I think, appreciated the holding and felt vindicated in her belief that unconventional relationships need that kind of community support. This is a belief that I also hold in my more balanced moments.

We had further check-ins through the week, often after dinner at her bungalow. It felt to me somewhat reminiscent of our time in ZEGG. It was clear to both of us that the second phase of our project was foundering; the container we created just weeks earlier had made little difference to the way I handled Saritha's romantic adventures. I was struggling as much with this most recent episode as I had in ZEGG. It was clear that my heart wasn't coping, but also, that I was also beginning to loose conviction. I was feeling that Saritha's experiments were undermining our relationship – indeed, dishonouring it. I told her that I wanted a relationship that was held more sacred than she appeared to hold ours. She argued that what she was doing was separate and distinct from our relationship and it carried no such implication. We were reaching an impasse and yet, I was still ambivalent. I found myself alternately wanting her and not wanting her, and the relationship. Poor thing, it must have been very confusing for her. It helped, of course, that she and her new friend had not sexualised their connection. Indeed, I found myself feeling grateful that she'd ended up bonding with a man who wasn't sexually available when it could so easily have been someone who was.

On the final night of the conference there was a dance. I had half a mind to skip it as I didn't want to see them dancing together and yet I could not. I went with a morbid masochistic compulsion that seemed very unlike me somehow – almost as if I was possessed. And things went downhill from there. I didn't handle the situation at all well. At one point I resorted to a low-grade stalking of Saritha around the dance floor. It was awful. I hated myself for it. Later that evening she agreed to a check-in. She was very reassuring, as she so assuredly can be. Indeed, she was extremely loving toward me, in both word and deed. Pacified, I headed home to bed, knowing that they were heading off together to an all-night after-party in his bungalow.

The next day I dropped him at the train station. In fact, he and I had got on extremely well over the week. We'd shared a beer at some point and formed a clear and honest understanding. Throughout this whole process I spent time thinking, mostly at night as I lay alone in bed, about my relationship and what it meant to me. I had reached a point of much greater self-awareness than at any point since Saritha and I came together almost six months earlier. The 'stalking incident,' as it laughingly became known to us, shook me to my core. It forced me to recognise my limerence for what it was (I'd rather call it that than addiction). And I resolved to address it, not just for her sake but, more importantly, for mine. Saritha wasn't so enamoured of my diagnosis. I think she saw it as demeaning of the essential or underlying source of my attraction. "Why can't you just see it as being in love?" she plaintively asked. But in any case, I had resolved to 'do some work on myself.' I called a therapist (for the first time in my life) and made an appointment for three weeks hence. And I registered for the introductory weekend of the *Mankind Project* in late November.

The week following the conference was very busy for us both. We had little time for each other and, in any case, little inclination to be together. We both needed down time. Toward the end of the week we held a check-in at Sunrise. We started, as we so often had done, with tension in the air. At one point, as we shared more and grew closer, we had the realisation that the love we had was as strong as ever. It was the rest of the shit going on between us that was the problem. In other words, the *relationship* was disrupting the love. So we made the simple choice to ditch the relationship altogether. We kissed as passionately as we had for two weeks and parted.

In the following week we had work to do together. Saritha was co-facilitating an ECL of two participants. It was to be held in the Park, which was unusual enough. But for someone who had only just completed ECL herself to be holding such a programme was rare indeed. I was very proud of her. To see her gaining recognition in the Foundation so rapidly was of no surprise to me, but a great joy nonetheless. I know what fulfilment she derives from group facilitation. I committed to helping her out by holding a couple of sessions myself.

Toward the end of the week, however, things went awry once more. Tension and irritation again entered our orbit.

THE END?

Late October, 2014

Back in September, I'd been lucky enough to gain a heavily subsidised place on a course in Esalen Massage starting on Saturday, October 18th.[1] I'd been looking forward to it for some time; I have always enjoyed giving and receiving massage. On the morning of the 18th, I went to Cluny where the course was being held, registered and moved into my room overlooking the gardens and golf course beyond.

Saturday evening is one of the two nights of the week when the sauna in Cluny is fired up. So after dinner, that's where I headed. And it was delicious. More than adequately hot, with a very cold outdoor plunge pool and a lovely wood-lined rest area, the Cluny sauna is a much valued facility, certainly by those hardcore sauna-goers who regularly meet there. I was returning to the sauna for the second or third time when something highly unexpected happened. I jumped up onto the top bench, diverting my eyes (as one does in a sauna) from the naked body of the woman I sat next too. "Hello," she said. My heart jumped at the sound of her voice;

---

[1] Esalen Massage is a style formulated at the well-known Esalen Institute and community in California. See http://www.esalen.org/.

it was Saritha.

We'd been having a challenging day; harsh (from me) and curt (from her) text messages had been flying back and forth between us. Before Saritha turned up, I'd been chatting with another beauty – a woman in whom I'd had an interest for some time. Indeed I'd have been showing her more attention much earlier, but for the fact that Saritha had always completely filled my field of view – satisfied me on every level, such that I had little interest in other women. But on this particular night, with communication between Saritha and I being so turgid, I found myself showing her considerable interest. However, when Saritha showed up, I was drawn back into our vortex of push-pull, attraction and repulsion.

By 10.30pm we were back at my place in The Park, processing the challenges of the previous few days. We were both feeling hurt and desperate. We talked for about an hour and decided that, once-and-for-all, we would split up – that our relationship wasn't serving either of us. Then we realised that in another half an hour, the date would be Oct 19th, exactly six months since we first got together. It seemed obvious that we should not formally split up before midnight. But, we asked, what to do with the remaining half hour? We decided to spend it in appreciation and celebration of our oftentimes joyous journey together. So we each shared what we'd most enjoyed about our adventures into love, sex and intimacy. And of course, in the process, we softened again and grew close. By midnight we were locked together passionately on the couch and deciding to spend the night together. However, the bedroom was so cold we decided to drag my extremely heavy latex mattress into the living room and sleep in front of the fire. In the morning we parted as singles, still fully resolved that the relationship was over, but knowing that we would likely remain lovers, albeit on an *ad hoc* basis. Essentially, we'd done what we'd discussed earlier – ditched the relationship in order to preserve the love. And it felt perfect!

In the days following, we held another leave-taking ritual much like the first. Rather than make macquettes, we wrote and drew on pieces of paper which we then burned in the wood stove. I was considerably more enthusiastic about this one; indeed, I instigated and organised it.

And so it was, through late October and into November, that we remained lovers on an *ad hoc* basis. Whether or not we were in relationship is moot. I think we both knew (even me) that any chance we had of making our relationship anything more committed or lasting, was long gone. We'd done our very best to overcome the essential differences between us, but ultimately, they were too great. Even I had become resigned to there being no future for us, perhaps not even as *ad hoc* lovers. In the periods in which we'd explored this option, I had struggled to remain detached. Even my newfound awareness of my patterns of addiction and attachment didn't seem to help, such is the power, it seems, of those devilish love hormones: Oxytocin, Vasopressin, Dopamine, etc.

Furthermore, we knew that Saritha was flying to Canada for three months on November 23rd and that almost certainly, she would drop off the radar during that period. I surmised that there was a good chance that I too would lose touch and begin to disconnect – I certainly hoped so. During the same period I'd be in Australia with family for six weeks. I'm going to feel fulfilled and loved up whilst there; my emotional needs will be well met without her. We have said that it makes no sense to entirely dismiss the possibility of re-engaging when Saritha returns in March. Why would we want to, indeed how could we, pre-empt the future? I think our chances are very slim, however. Three months is a long time when one lives and loves as passionately as we both do.

IONA

Early November 2014

Some months earlier, we had planned a trip together – a week away on the mystical Isle of Iona on the West Coast of Scotland. I had seen it as celebratory *finale* to our time together. However, as the time approached and we struggled to hold our relationship together, we asked each other, "Will we still go to Iona?" And every time, we decided, "Yes, we will, *regardless!*" Especially after we'd chosen to step out of the relationship and just be occasional lovers, the Iona trip didn't seem right somehow. It was always going to be challenging, being domestic for a whole week, particularly if the weather kept us indoors. Yet, we remained determined to go; we were both so looking forward to it. I'd been there before and absolutely loved it. Saritha had never been there, but was equally strongly drawn to go.

So it was that on November 8th, Saritha and I left Findhorn with another friend to spend a week in *Traigh Bhan*, a cosy three bedroom retreat house belonging to the Findhorn Foundation. It's situated fifty metres from the waters of the Sound of Mull at the north end of Iona. We departed at 5.30am on the Saturday morning. The six hour bus ride across Scotland from east to west was spectacular. Three ferry rides induced in me a growing sense of remoteness from work and community life. We were excited and arrived at the house full of expectation. Symbolically, it is one of the few houses I've ever seen without even a path to the door, let alone any road access. The only approach is by foot over cow paddocks or by boat from the ocean. What a perfect setting for a retreat house.

The first hiccup (as far as I was concerned) occurred five minutes after we arrived when Saritha decided to sleep downstairs in the bunk room rather than upstairs with me in a beautiful double bedroom overlooking the water. I was hurt, but not surprised; we were after all, officially no longer in a relationship. Later that day we had a silly tiff, probably as a result of the hurt, but a late night walk on the beach in the moonlight brought us close again. The views of the moon reflecting off the water were spectacular. We had fun with some moonlit photography and soon enough, Saritha pulled me toward a jagged rock for some rather uncomfortable light-hearted kissing and cuddling. We wandered back to the house in each other's arms, went to bed and made love in my room with the moonlight streaming through the windows above us. Saritha then went downstairs to sleep.

Sunday was brilliantly sunny – the only day of sunshine we had. The only day without rain and wind. Saritha and I took a long walk up the highest hill on the island and across some rocky marshland to a spectacular beach of sand, pebbles and rocky outcrops. The evocative landscape and sunshine left us feeling high on nature and the wild remoteness of the island. We didn't see another person (until the very end when we were unfairly accused of trespassing by a grumpy homeowner). There was a memorable quality to the walk; it induced a different kind of intimacy between us. In the evening, I gave Saritha a massage as her legs were hurting from the exercise. We made more love that night – again with a view of the moonlight reflecting off the water. We slept together; rising early to meditate in the beautiful wee sanctuary at the top of the stairs.

The following day was wet and windy. At one point we

found ourselves in the front porch with the rain beating against the windows and skylights. The porch is my favourite room in the house. With windows wrapped around three sides and extra large skylights, it's a space that's filled with light and views to the water, garden and the fields all around. It's almost possible to feel that one is actually outdoors and immersed in nature.

With our fondness for making love in nature, Saritha and I found ourselves drawn to the day bed at one end of the porch. It's a bed that's used for napping during the day, and in summer as an extra night-time sleeping option. I doubt it's used very much for lovemaking, because it is so public. That however, didn't stop us, even though our housemate was around and might have walked in at any time. We cuddled under a blanket and then discreetly removed just sufficient clothing to enable union to occur. With the sound of the rain and wind on the glass all around us, we were once again transported to that place we love so much, where human sensuality and love of nature merge together.

That night, just before bed, I experienced a rare desire to sleep alone and to not make love. I was feeling sated and a little tired from all of the sexual activity of the previous days. I asked Saritha if this would be ok with her. She smiled at me and agreed. However, within half an hour she'd crawled into my bed and was initiating sex – at least that's my recollection. I think she might argue otherwise, but it felt to me that, by pulling back rather than pushing for intimacy as I would normally do, I had triggered a reaction in her – she'd come toward me, seeking engagement. Anyway, we made love again that night. And in the morning we pushed our boundaries just that little bit further with some beautiful anal sex. We were lying on our sides, looking into each other's eyes. The pain and ecstasy we shared flowed like a river between us. It left us feeling very, very close for most of the day. However, toward evening, irritations arose once more and by the end of the day we were both ready for a night off. I slept on my own, like a log.

The following day, Wednesday, was again wet and windy. We were forced to stay indoors to our increasing frustration. In the morning, however, we found time to sit together under a blanket in the porch and digitally record our recollections of the previous three month's journeying together. It is that recording which has informed the writing of the last third of this book.

When the rain subsided in the late afternoon, Saritha and I ventured out for a walk to the Abbey. I'd been there many times and was keen to share its unique qualities with her. We got there at 4.30pm – closing time. Undeterred, we entered in the failing light to find the church and cloister seemingly abandoned, but for the distant sound of choral singing creeping out from under a thick wooden door. We sat in the church, in silence and semi-darkness, soaking up the mediaeval atmosphere. In fact, we barely exchanged a word during the visit or on the way home, when once again, the wind and rain returned. By the time we got back to *Traigh Bhan*, we both had rivulets of icy water running down the insides of our not-so-waterproof jackets. We went to bed together that night. Our lovemaking was, for once, uninspired. Saritha had developed a chill by this time and was sneezing throughout. And I was feeling disconnected. The following day, I described it as 'second-rate sex', much to Saritha's dismay.

The rain and wind continued unabated. By now our wee house was feeling too small, even for just three of us. (It can sleep up to 10). It felt like a prison and I was beginning to feel more than a little stir crazy. So it was that in the late evening, I went completely crazy. Saritha wanted to sleep on her own again. I went to bed feeling rejected. I couldn't sleep. Rejection turned to abandonment as my inner child threw a tantrum. At one point, around 2am, I went downstairs and crept into her room, without much of a plan. Saritha wakened. She laughed quietly in the darkness and compassionately invited me into her narrow single bed. She held and stroked me, beautifully role playing the mother from whom my inner child was feeling so separated. Later, seeking greater comfort, we went upstairs to my bed where we continued to cuddle. For once, I had no desire to make love. I was feeling too vulnerable.

Friday was our last full day on the Island. We busied ourselves with tasks around the house and so the continuing bad weather went generally unnoticed. However, I was aware that this was the final opportunity for Saritha and I to complete. She had one more week to spend back in Findhorn before flying off to Canada. I had unilaterally decided, even before coming to Iona, that it would be best if we completed our time together on the island, rather than struggle to satisfactorily do so whilst she was preoccupied with wrapping up her busy work and social life. So when it came time for bed, I was keen for us to spend one final night together. I didn't want our final lovemaking, either in experience or memory, to be 'second-rate.' She was reluctant, but mindful of the tantrum of the night before, and thus agreed. And I think she wanted it too.

We both really enjoyed what I was convinced would be our final night together. We cuddled and talked. Our lovemaking was slow, gentle and sweet. And in the morning, as she still dozed, I ritualistically said goodbye to Saritha's perfect body, part-by-part, as both an act of appreciation and a way (I hoped) of finally cutting the cords of attachment. The day dawned sunny and warm. Finally, good weather had returned to the island on the day we were leaving. Nonetheless, it raised our spirits. We left the house, walked to the ferry and crossed the Sound of Mull in good cheer. We took photos, sat in the sun in each other's arms and sang Beatles songs whilst waiting for the bus. I was contented and at peace. I was feeling ready to release Saritha forever.

OUR FINAL WEEK

Mid November 2014

The title of this chapter is a spoiler. It carries the implication that we spent Saritha's final week at Findhorn back together. Else it might have been titled 'The Final Week' or perhaps this book might have ended with the previous chapter. So what did we do together in that final week, given that we'd completed and released each other on Iona? Well, I'd say, we did everything! Our final week together was like an encapsulation of our entire seven month long journey.

Actually, we were always going to have to engage on some, albeit perfunctory, level. I had committed to supporting Saritha with her preparations for leaving. At the very least, I was going to take her shopping for gifts, help her to organise her packing, store some of her stuff and take her to the airport. But when we left Iona, this was the only engagement I was expecting. I was determined not to seek or demand her time or attention, which is the way it was for the first few days. We met a few times in the CC or at Sunrise in order to organise what needed to be done, but there was no emotional, and very little physical, engagement – a parting hug perhaps, but certainly not a kiss. We were both very clear that we weren't going to go there.

On Wednesday, Saritha told me that she was having

dinner with a mutual friend that night. Uh-oh, I thought, here we go again; she'll end up cuddling and kissing with him for sure. I knew that the two of them had enjoyed a mutual attraction for some months. They had acknowledged and talked about it but, as far as I know, had not acted on the attraction much at all. So I couldn't help but think, knowing her as I do, that they would push the limits as far as possible. I knew he had a committed but open relationship with a woman who happened to be away at the time and, depending on what their particular agreements were, there would be a limit to what was acceptable to him. Having fully completed with me, Saritha would have no such self-imposed restrictions, but I knew she would respect his choices, of course.

So it was that early on Thursday morning she told me of their adventures of the previous evening. She and I had arranged days earlier to meet at my place at 8.00am that day, so that she could do some packing and for us to go shopping in the nearby city of Elgin. She duly showed up at 8.05 and immediately spilled the beans. She'd gone to his place for dinner, walked back to the Park with him and then gone for a late night hot tub. In the tub (the same place where she and I enjoyed our first physical contact) they got creative with a block of chocolate, using it as body paint and then licking it off (from which body parts, she didn't say). They had then kissed, but had gone no further, Saritha said. That was the limit of the agreement he had with his partner.

Well, I thought, that went according to the script; I wasn't at all surprised. Furthermore, I wasn't greatly triggered, in good part because I'd genuinely released Saritha from any commitment to me. I saw her as an entirely free agent. And perhaps I was less triggered, because I love the guy as a friend. Somehow, that made it easier to be less jealous of him.

We headed off to Elgin around 9am, did some shopping and returned to my place around 11. Then something extraordinary happened. I still have no idea what it was that catalysed the shift, but without doubt, there was a huge shift of attitude and energy in Saritha. Perhaps it was something to do with her date of the previous evening and/or my relaxed response to it. Perhaps it was due to the activities of the morning or perhaps it was due to her realising that her departure was imminent – I really have no idea. It began as we sat on the couch with a cup of tea. Within seconds we were locked in a passionate embrace, kissing as if there was no tomorrow (which, in a sense, was the case). Within minutes we were lying together on the couch experiencing some of the most highly charged and erotic exchanges of energy of our entire seven months together. Ripples of orgasmic energy coursed in unison through our bodies – building to a crescendo and subsiding and building again, time after time. I was reminded of the period we spent together at the very beginning of our journey, before Saritha went to Brighton. It was as much of a revelation as that, but had an infinitely deeper and richer quality, because of the subsequent deepening of our love. All of this was happening whilst we were fully clothed. In fact, it was happening without very much physical touching, stroking or kissing. For the most part, we were simply looking deeply into each other's eyes, *beholding*. It felt truly sacred. It felt to me as if a river of pure love was flowing between us, not so much from heart-to-heart but via our eyes to and from the deepest parts of us – our very souls. For me, it was yet another new consciousness-expanding experience. I was incredulous.

Our clothed lovemaking continued for close to two hours before we realised that it was lunchtime. I had no food in the house and neither of us wanted to break the spell by having to go to the Community Centre to eat. So I left her on the couch and went to fetch food for us both. We enjoyed a meal together and resumed our energetic exchange. Saritha's period had arrived the previous day so there was an extra reason for not removing our clothes and engage sexually. But in actual fact, we were very much enjoying the deep energetic and sensual exchange for it not being sexual. Eventually however, I was the one who succumbed to my most basic of urges and Saritha obliged with some expert fellatio.

We eventually went to dinner in the CC and returned to my place in the early evening. We'd planned for me to give Saritha a massage and for us to have an early night. It was clear that we were going to spend the night together, despite our decision on Iona not to do so again. Saritha was a little ambivalent as she hates to go back on agreements. I was grateful for our flexibility. Anyway, she got busy with some work she needed to do, backing up her computer before leaving. By the time she'd finished, the time was 11pm and we decided to forgo the massage and head for bed. I gave her a lesser massage there, not the full featured Esalen treatment that I'd planned. We made love – not penetratively, but fabulously nonetheless.

We rose early the next day, Friday, and meditated. Saritha was wrapped in the blanket I'd bought her in Elgin the previous day. Through my eyes, as I sat opposite her, she looked more beautiful than ever; my appreciation of her physical beauty seemed to have deepened somehow. This gentle, nourishing beginning to her final day in Findhorn lent a soft, open-heartedness to our mood. We kissed and kissed again as we prepared to leave the house. It was going to be a busy day for us both. I spent the morning running errands for her. She made progress sorting out her stuff. She had to vacate Sunrise before leaving so thought it best to move her belongings to my place and finally sort and pack them there.

We connected at lunchtime in the Community Centre. But, as I was leaving the CC, I saw her and her date of two evenings prior standing with their arms wrapped around each other. I sensed a sadness about their embrace; perhaps it was to be their last meeting before she left. Something moved inside of me – I suppose it was caring, compassion or love; I'm not sure. But I was drawn to go to them both and hug them and to say a few words of appreciation to him for helping me work on my jealousy issues. I told them that I was feeling much less jealous than I might have expected, because I liked him so much. Saritha was touched. She purred with delight. I imagined that this was what she'd sought all along – to be able to maintain a relationship with me whilst exploring with another; and to do so with grace and acceptance. I left wondering whether we might not have just glimpsed the unconditional love to which Saritha and I once aspired.

At dinner, about a dozen of Saritha's friends gathered around a table in the CC to bid her farewell. We followed up with some dancing, which lasted less than an hour. We had further options for the evening: to see a film in the Universal Hall or go with friends to the pub? But we decided that a massage and an early night was much more appealing. So that's what we did. We picked up the last of Saritha's belongings at Sunrise and headed home. Unlike the previous evening, there was no work to be done; Saritha didn't even turn on her computer. Instead, she headed off for a shower whilst I busied myself setting up the massage table. I eventually joined her in the shower, wondering why she was taking so long. I noticed her shaver there and surmised that she'd done what she did once before – shaved herself 'for me,' as she said later. What gratitude and joy I felt, not so much for the act itself, but for her motivation. She was expressing a love for me in action that perhaps she wouldn't allow herself to express in words.

She fell asleep during the massage. A good sign I thought; an indication of her happy and relaxed state of mind – free from concern, criticism and doubt. Afterwards we went to bed and made love for what I thought (yet again) would be the last time. Our lovemaking was truly sacred that night – slow and gentle, and infused in every single moment with divine love. We didn't lose eye contact, except momentarily, despite adopting several different positions. We drifted off to sleep with my arms wrapped tightly around her as she murmured endearing appreciations. My last thoughts were of appreciation too, that the memory of our exquisite lovemaking, our last, would linger in my cellular memory for weeks, perhaps months, to come.

Little did I know of what was to follow on our final day.

OUR FINAL DAY

November 23rd, 2014

Once again, we rose early to meditate. There was still much to be done. Saritha hadn't fully sorted her things, separating what she wanted to take to Canada from what she would leave with me to store. She set about doing this, using the massage table for layout whilst I made porridge. We sat on the couch to have breakfast, but struggled to focus on eating. We were both feeling horny – very horny. The sexual energy we were feeling was different from the night before – less sacred and more carnal, more wanton. Impressively, we decided that there was just too much to do to get diverted at this point. So we broke away from one another and Saritha continued her packing, leaving me to clean up the house. "I don't think we've made love for the final time," she said, with a smile. For the next two hours we did what was necessary, but were completely distracted by the desire we both felt. We came together several times more for some deeply passionate and erotic kissing and clinching.

Finally, we completed the tasks of the morning and took a final shower together. We hadn't often made love in the shower – only once, I think, on the floor, way back at the beginning of our sexual exploration. This was to be the second time and we did it standing up, or at least, I was standing as I lifted Saritha from the floor and she wrapped her legs around my waist. We were as abandoned in our lovemaking as at any time in the previous seven months, completely lost in a haze of desire. It was wondrous.

Soon after, we packed the car and headed to Sunrise for some last minute sorting of Saritha's art and craft materials. She did that as I grabbed some lunch from the kitchen. We headed back to the car where a few friends had gathered for final hugs and farewells. We left for the airport with Saritha feeding me roast potatoes and salad with her fingers, which I nipped and licked in return. It took us half of the journey to have lunch. During the remainder of the time, Saritha leaned over and performed on me what's commonly referred to in the newspapers as 'a sex act.' We had to curtail the activity when we got to the airport, which left us both feeling dangerously horny.

She checked in as I scouted for somewhere with privacy. I had in mind a disabled toilet and sure enough found one that would suit. As soon as she'd dropped her rucksack, we embarked on what would undoubtedly be our final erotic adventure. We entered the toilet together, not caring if we'd been spotted doing so, locked the door and in a frenzy of kissing, ripped the clothing from the lower half of each other's bodies. Saritha rode me as I sat on the pedestal, first facing toward me then away. Finding this awkward, we stood with her hanging onto the basin and me entering her from behind. This worked fabulously, not least because we could maintain eye contact and watch each other's facial expressions in the mirror. This was one occasion when I wasn't going to wait for her to have her usual three orgasms before I had mine; I was going for it! I came in minutes. She almost did. We dressed, left the room together, again without caring who saw us, and headed for the departure gate in a state of exhilaration. We smiled in silent acknowledgement of the inner adventurer in each other and the enjoyment of pushing the boundaries of our sexual exploration just that little bit further. We kissed for the final time and Saritha headed toward the rather stern looking official at the gate.

I think I smiled all the way home, not least due to the several saucy text messages that flew between us as I drove and she waited in the departure lounge. I had to pull over three or four times to read and reply. 'Nice to think of you journeying with a little bit of me inside of you,' I wrote. 'I just finished myself off in the toilet,' she replied.

What an incredible woman I thought. What a sexual diva!

AFTERWORD

December 2014

Saritha has been gone for over a month now. For a few days following her departure I remained in a fog of joy and wonder at what transpired in our final days together. But I had work to do – a busy week at work tying up loose ends before leaving for Australia followed by an intensive two-day workshop with the Mankind Project. I'm not at liberty to reveal much of what transpired on the MKP weekend. Suffice to say that it involved deep shadow work and processes based on the same Jungian archetypes that I discussed in the chapter titled, *On Archetypes*. As a result of that work, plus the benefit of distance and a month's reflection, I've resolved to be more true to myself in the future.

I feel that there was something quite dysfunctional about the way our experiment in free love unfolded. I was hurt too deeply, too often. Admittedly, a good part of the cause was my judgment about the nature of Saritha's exploration with other men. Her adventures appeared to me to be too circumstantial, too arbitrary, and too impulsive. My limerence and plain old fashioned jealousy were also at fault. I take full responsibility for all these sources of my own pain (judgment, limerence and jealousy) and readily admit that they are all quite futile emotional conditions.

However, I feel that both Saritha and I could have done more to limit the collateral damage; we could have better applied the principles we established for that purpose. With the benefit of this experience, I'd now seek a relationship that held kindness and respect paramount. That is not to say that it need be exclusive or monogamous. But if not, then when not, I'd wish for much greater caring and consideration for the feelings of the other than either of us demonstrated at times during those last few months.

And what will become of the love? Saritha was my portal into connection with the divine – most often experienced through our lovemaking, but that wasn't its only manifestation. I've made many references to my love feeling boundless; which has been my experience of it at times. There have been moments where I've felt like love itself – a transcendent and mystical kind of love. I know with absolute certainty that my love for Saritha will not subside. My hope is that it continues to transmute into the unconditional love that I glimpsed in the days before she left. That aside, my love for Saritha will always be available to her in whatever way serves us both.

Whatever the future brings, I will remain deeply grateful for the amazing journey we took together over those seven months in 2014. I believe that Saritha and I achieved what we set out to do. We not only met, but we danced, in that field that lies 'out beyond ideas of wrongdoing and rightdoing'. And in so doing, I was transformed. The experience, growth and learning I gained were immeasurable; I am a changed man. Furthermore, we succeeded as planned, to document our project and disseminate the findings of our 'research'. We thank you, the reader, for participating in that process and hope that this book will inform and inspire your own adventures in loving.

Thank you, beloved.

Thank you, Beloved.

Graham

POSTSCRIPT

June, 2015

Six months have passed since Saritha left Findhorn and five since this book was first published. Much has happened in that time, enough to warrant a reissuing of the book (not a second edition, as such, but a minor revision) and the addition of this postscript. I thought readers might be interested in an update.

After Saritha departed for Canada, we maintained steady contact for a month or so, mostly emailing about details of this book leading up to its publication. Following that, contact became less frequent. She was travelling in Canada; I was travelling in Australia. Eventually we lost contact entirely. As predictable as this was, it was difficult for me to accept. I thought I had emotionally released her and processed my attachment, but the events of our final two days together had put paid to that. The deep energetic exchange of the second last day and passionate send-off at the airport had deeply imprinted on my mind's eye. I yearned for her, and for connection. Saritha, on the other hand, just wanted to get on with her adventures in Canada. Our different needs and wants spawned several fractious emails. Then, a particularly vacuous Skype call convinced me that it was finally all over between us. Her heart seemed tightly shut. Soon after, Saritha announced that 'new love was growing.' I wasn't as thrown by this as I might have expected. In fact, I was relieved; a new relationship would surely put an end to the push-pull, start-stop dynamic of ours, once and for all.

Saritha arrived back in Findhorn at the end of February. There'd been no contact between us for weeks. I'd withdrawn my standing offer to pick her up at the airport so we first met in the CC at a crowded community event. It reminded me of the first time we had reconnected at ZEGG back in July. She seemed demonstrably more interested in connecting with others than with me. We exchanged a few words and a cursory hug; that was all. It was clear to us both that we needed to process so the next day we agreed to meet at my place for a chat, debrief, check-in, I wasn't sure what exactly. We met once and then on a second occasion without making much headway; the disconnection between us seemed insurmountable. Our third and final attempt to find some peace and reconciliation was a supervised meeting attended by a mutual friend. On this occasion, tears flowed. Saritha expressed a heart-felt need for 'space.' I was able to soften and hear her, so agreed to the request. We went our separate ways and didn't much speak to each other for weeks, which stretched into months.

Looking back as I write this, I can see all too clearly just how reactive and immature was much of our behaviour of this period; how far we had fallen from the high aspirations we set in our first Dreaming almost a year earlier. Our conscious relationship had become a totally dysfunctional one. However, separate and different life-changing events were about to overtake us both. I was to embark on a journey into Tantra; Saritha was to deepen into a brand new and potentially much more promising relationship.

In early March I undertook a week long, intensive Tantra training for beginners held at Newbold House. I am not at liberty to reveal much about the course due to an informal non-disclosure agreement. But, in any case, reading about it would not in the slightest way convey the experience. Such a journey of initiation can only be understood in the doing and the experiencing. Apart from that, knowing about the content in advance would spoil the experience for anyone who subsequently decided to do such a workshop. At no time during the week were we given a schedule or otherwise told of what was coming next. And that in itself was powerful. Each new step in the journey was a complete surprise. The unfolding of the experience felt like being led on a magical mystery tour.

Five Findhorn Foundation coworkers attended the course, which for me was another special dimension of the experience i.e. undertaking a journey of profound personal discovery with fellow community members. We deepened our connection immeasurably. And in the case of one guy in particular, he and I established a heart connection where before there was only distance and resistance between us. In fact, by the end of the week I was left feeling totally in love with everyone, everything, indeed the whole damned universe! I understood the sacredness of all life and unity of everything. I genuinely felt that 'all that I am, is one with all that is,' a phrase repeatedly invoked during the course.

On the evening following the end of the course I went with a friend to see the Scottish Ballet perform Tennessee Williams' Streetcar Named Desire, a classic story of love, desire and sexuality. In my heightened state of sensitivity to exactly these aspects of our common humanity, I was totally transfixed and moved by the performance. Gore Vidal said of the original play that it 'changed the concept of sex in America.' How synchronistic that I should attend such a performance the day after completing a Tantra initiation. For I believe the course has likewise changed my conception of my own sexuality. I learned an enormous amount through the week, about my long-held sexual attitudes, preoccupations and patterns. Some of the lessons were hard, but all the more beneficial for that. And some of the experience was truly transformative and inspiring. Three months on, the changes in consciousness have stayed with me. I'm more grounded, present and centered. I'm much less driven than before – calmer, clearer and more confident somehow. In respect of Saritha, I'm cured of my heart's limerence and exaggerated sexual desire for her. I have released her energetically and blessed her on her journey.

Whilst all this was unfolding for me, Saritha was deepening into her newfound love for a man she met in Canada. Within weeks of her arrival back in Findhorn her lover had come for a short visit then gone on to Germany where he is based. I met him briefly on the street outside my house. I liked him immediately; he had an open, affable demeanour. No jealousy arose in me, just a heartfelt wish for the success of their union. Soon after that, Saritha travelled to be with him for a short holiday. Their relationship was deep and meaningful, she told me upon her return, but it was also challenging; there were significant differences between them. It was clear to me that she truly loved him; I heard it in her words and saw it in her expression. I felt very happy for her. I sensed that the 'differences' might enable her to soften, learn and grow in ways that she was not able to do with me.

Some weeks ago, Saritha's lover returned to Findhorn for a longer visit. This time, he and I had more opportunity to meet and get to know each other. We enjoyed the contact and discovered commonalities, not least a love of sport, golf in particular. I invited him for a game at one of the numerous courses nearby. We enjoyed a leisurely round, chatting and deepening our connection. I could feel a friendship beginning to build. By the time he left to return to Germany we had grown quite close. On the day before he was about to leave, I offered to take him to the train station. Unexpectedly, they both turned up at my place early the next morning; Saritha had decided to come too. We got there 15 minutes early and stood on the platform, the three of us, chatting quietly. It was a sweet, if not somewhat ironic, moment. On the way home, Saritha and I chatted happily. We acknowledged that the growing friendship between her lover and I had softened the space between us. We felt as relaxed and at ease with each other as at any time since her leaving in November.

So what have been the lessons learned in the last six months since publication? What realisations have I had with the benefit of hindsight, distance and time? What additional reflections can be added to those of the Afterword? Well, they fall roughly into two types – those about the relationship itself and those which might be called meta-reflections about the very nature of love, sexuality and intimacy, which is to say, about being human. On the first type, feedback from readers of this book has been instructive. Everyone I've heard from, without exception, loved the first half of the book – the honeymoon phase. I guess that might mean that romanticism is alive and well in the 21st C. But opinion was divided, roughly 50-50, over the second half of the story – the slow degradation of our relationship, the serial breaking up and making up. Some readers, particularly those attempting polyamorous arrangements, derived huge benefit; they felt affirmed, relieved and reassured that they are not alone with their relationship challenges. Others simply enjoyed reading a true story about an intense, ardent relationship between two quite ordinary people. They appreciated the honesty, transparency and authenticity of it, particularly because such stories are so rarely published. However, a roughly equal number of readers found the second half of the book distressing. And here, I have to admit, I can understand their response. The way that Saritha and I treated each other in those last few months was regrettable, if not deplorable. It was violent, in a passive aggressive kind of way. And we were equally responsible. With the benefit of six months of distance from events, I can admit now to being as capable as her of unkind and disrespectful behaviour. This doesn't come across in the book because it was written from my immersive personal perspective at the time. But I recognise my culpability now and have recently been able to admit it, both to myself and to Saritha.

That said, the questions I've asked myself repeatedly over the last six months are less about the detail of our relationship and more about the nature of the attraction between us and of love itself. Did I really love Saritha, or was it simply deep sexual attraction? I can unequivocally say that it felt like love at the time; indeed, it felt like the love of my life. I can remember saying on several occasions during our first few months together that I would have married her in an instant. However, I now realise that my desire was being almost entirely hormonally driven by sexual attraction and gratification. That's not to say that I didn't love her; I did, simply because that's what it felt like at the time. Love comes in infinite variations and this was one of them. Of course it wasn't a deep or enduring love. But it was love of sorts. And even now, despite the many challenges, I care for her deeply and about her wellbeing. This too, feels like love of a kind. It seems that we need as many words to describe love as do the Inuit to describe snow.

I would also like to acknowledge the sexual journey we took together which, for me, was truly profound. Having spent my whole adult life being so sexually driven and fascinated by all things erotic, to be with a woman who could meet me there (in that field out beyond etc. etc.) was truly liberating. Saritha took me places I hadn't been even in my imagination. Our lovemaking transformed my relationship to my sexuality in much the same way that the Tantra course has done more recently. Both have brought lasting peace and true sexual healing.

Sexuality is important to us all. We are hard wired for sexual desire in order that our species is perpetuated. Indeed all life is driven to procreate. Life begets life. Humans, of course, have almost uniquely evolved to be able to separate sex and procreation. (I say almost uniquely because Bonobo monkeys and I believe a few other species also recreate sexually.) And yet, despite sexuality being the life force of our species and central to our wellbeing as individuals, we struggle to talk about it. We struggle to talk about it and we struggle to express it, even privately, let alone publicly. The taboos around sexuality in contemporary society are such that it takes quite some courage to venture beyond the norms. And, I would suggest, even more so within the context of community. After any 'coming out' (as gay, poly, or any other variation from the norm) a 'field' or network of support is essential for the well-being of the individuals concerned. Which was precisely the motivation behind the recent forming of a group called 'Healing Love and Sexuality Findhorn' (HLSF). Comprising about 20 members, the group meets weekly for a range of different activities, most of which involve 'sharing' what's going on for us in the realm of love, sexuality and intimacy.

I'm not going to enter into a cultural analysis here, but I think it is clear even without substantiation that sexual thoughts, feelings and behaviours are repressed and sublimated in our Western, Christian, post-Victorian, middle class culture, and most elsewhere else as well. And most of us are frustrated, unfulfilled and/or damaged as a result. Our HLSF group has arisen from the deep need that most of us carry to heal the wounds this creeping catastrophe has caused. Our meetings provide an outlet and a forum for the expression of long suppressed thoughts, feelings and behaviours. Recent meetings have been truly liberating. In the last few weeks I have witnessed some deep and courageous sharing from participants as they open wounds (that in many cases they've been carrying for a lifetime) in order that healing and transformation may begin. This has been particularly inspiring for me as someone who so strongly believes in the value of transparency.

I'd like to conclude by returning to my personal journey. I have spent the last six months being single and effectively celibate. However, I've been blessed during this period with a surfeit of love and intimacy. Without a narrow focus on relationship with one person, I've deepened my connections with many friends (men, as well as women); I have felt deeply nurtured and cared for. And in respect of women, I now have numerous very loving but platonic relationships that I didn't have six months ago. I can only imagine that my being less sexually driven, with a newfound inner stillness and sense of self, has enabled the building of trust and therefore intimacy.

Without the distraction of a relationship, I've also been able to get on with my various projects, one of which was the publication of another book titled, 'Findhorn Reflections: A very personal take on life inside the famous spiritual community and ecovillage.' My work in the Conference Office of the Foundation has been enjoyably manic. We have a major conference coming up – the GEN+20 Summit. GEN (the Global Ecovillage Network) is an international umbrella organisation representing thousands of ecovillages in more than 100 countries. In early July several hundred delegates and general participants will descend on Findhorn for a celebration of GEN's 20th anniversary. The logistics of this event have been my main preoccupation of the last several months.

So life goes on. In November I hope to deepen further into Tantra with a follow-up week-long workshop being held in Somerset. And on the day the course finishes, I'll board a plane to Australia to spend the summer there with family and meet my third grandchild. As I write these words I am filled with love and gratitude for family, friends, community, my life here in Findhorn and not least, for the deepening into love, sex and intimacy that has been gifted me over the last twelve months.

With love,
Graham

ABOUT THE AUTHOR

As a teenager, I began a life-long search for an alternative lifestyle that would enable me to live congruently with my communitarian values, dreams and aspirations. The journey took me initially to kibbutz in Israel (for three years) then to a Australia's largest hippie commune (for eight years). Later, as an architect and academic, I extensively researched and wrote about ecovillages and cohousing communities all around the world. For the last ten years I've lived very contentedly in the famous spiritual community and ecovillage in Findhorn, North Scotland.

Other books by Graham Meltzer
(all available on Amazon)

Another Kind of Space:
Creating Ecological Dwellings and Environments (2003)
(co-authored with Alan Dearling)

Sustainable Community:
Learning from the Cohousing Model (2005)

Findhorn Reflections: A very personal take on life inside the
famous spiritual community and ecovillage (2015)